# Hope That Goes the Distance

Also by Jud Wilhite

*Faith That Goes the Distance: Living an Extraordinary Life*
*Love That Goes the Distance: Discover the Power That*
*  Conquers All*

What people are saying about Jud Wilhite's series:

*Faith That Goes the Distance* is an intelligent, clever, and explosive exploration of faith's power. This book speaks to the heart with wisdom and humor. Get ready to be moved as well as inspired!

BARRY MCMURTRIE, SENIOR PASTOR,
CROSSROADS CHRISTIAN CHURCH

This book will remind you of how God can use absolutely anyone to glorify his kingdom. Jud makes it clear, through God's Word, that you don't have to be a figure of prominence for your faith to make a difference in the lives of others. If you are willing to do the natural by taking a stand for Christ and becoming obedient to his Word, Christ will bless you with the super and lead others closer to him.

BRANDON SLAY, U.S. OLYMPIC GOLD MEDALIST

Directly ties the faith of the "giants of the Bible" with the "giants" that live among us today, and encourages us toward that same exercise of faith. *Faith That Goes the Distance* was worth the wait!

UPBEAT REPORTER

Jud Wilhite puts forth a clear and inspirational plan for how to live an extraordinary adventure with God. Filled with powerful stories of how God works through every day people, *Faith That Goes the Distance* will challenge you to take a risk and discover life's greatest rewards.

MIKE FOSTER, CO-FOUNDER OF XXXCHURCH.COM

After reading *Love That Goes the Distance*, my life will never be the same—and neither will yours. This is the book I've been waiting to read my entire life, and Jud Wilhite has finally written it.

PAT WILLIAMS, SR. VICE PRESIDENT, ORLANDO MAGIC,
AUTHOR OF *HOW TO BE LIKE JESUS*

Love . . . we all express it on a daily basis, but what about when it's hard to do? What about the unlovely, the lonely, the discouraged, and those requiring forgiveness? Jud Wilhite, in his insightful book *Love That Goes the Distance*, empowers us to love when it's not easy by learning from real life experiences and Bible characters who can teach us valuable lessons.

BOB RUSSELL, SENIOR MINISTER,
SOUTHEAST CHRISTIAN CHURCH

Some communicators have tremendous handle on their subject matter. Others are adept at translating their subject into the language of their audience. Jud Wilhite does both with precision and passion. I predict you will be giving this book away often to friends who need to be reminded of the power of supernatural love.

GENE APPEL, ASSOCIATE PASTOR,
WILLOW CREEK COMMUNITY CHURCH

*Love That Goes the Distance* left me wanting more. Not because it was empty of meaning but rather because it was full of encouraging insights that actually could help me "go the distance." Jud Wilhite has taken God's truths written thousands of years ago and spilled light on them, exposing God's love that has the power to transform our lives.

GREG NETTLE, SENIOR PASTOR,
RIVERTREE CHRISTIAN CHURCH

From cover to cover, *Love That Goes the Distance* captures the essence of Christ's love for people. It delivers a powerful message of grace, love, and hope to the sensitive seeker and the discouraged disciple. An inspirational read no matter where you are on the journey of life. In an era of broken promises and failed relationships, *Love That Goes the Distance* reminds us of the sustaining love relationship that God wants with each of us found in Jesus Christ.

CHAPLAIN RAYMOND GIUNTA,
EXECUTIVE DIRECTOR/FOUNDER OF WE CARE MINISTRIES

This book is a resource for pastors. Every chapter includes well-selected powerful quotes. But the most inspiring thing about *Love That Goes the Distance* is Jud's attitude. He cheers for other people by magnifying their stories and celebrating what God has done for them.

DR. SARAH SUMNER, CHAIR OF THE MINISTRY DEPARTMENT,
AZUSA PACIFIC UNIVERSITY

# HOPE THAT GOES THE DISTANCE

*Experiencing God's Future Today*

## JUD WILHITE

BakerBooks

Grand Rapids, Michigan

Published by Baker Books
a division of Baker Publishing Group
P.O. Box 6287, Grand Rapids, MI 49516-6287
www.bakerbooks.com

Printed in the United States of America

Library of Congress Cataloging-in-Publication Data
Wilhite, Jud, 1971–
    Hope that goes the distance : experiencing God's future today / Jud Wilhite.
        p.     cm.
    Includes bibliographical references.
    ISBN 0-8010-6463-5 (pbk.)
        1. Hope—Religious aspects—Christianity. 2. Faith—Biblical teaching. 3. Bible—Criticism, interpretation, etc.  I. Title.
    BV4638.W54 2004
    234'.25—dc22                                              2004003913

To Ethan
May hope sustain you on the journey

# CONTENTS

# ACKNOWLEDGMENTS

Where there is life, there is hope," the saying goes, but I tend to believe that where there is hope, there is life, which is why I'm so grateful to the many people who have inspired hope in me, especially Lori, Emma, and Ethan. Thank you for sharing me with a laptop for countless hours to complete this book.

Many opened their lives for these pages; thanks for allowing us to be motivated by your hope. To my friends who keep hope alive, your encouragement is invaluable —Jon Bodin, Mike Bodine, Jayson French, Mike Foster, Dave Gothi, Scott Greer, Peter McGowan, Mel McGowan, Ray Guinta, Barry McMurtrie, Michael Murphy, Greg Nettle, Bart Rendel, Geoff Sage, Paul Trainor, Mark Welchel, and Shawn Williams.

Thanks to Eugena Kelting who does an amazing job of keeping my life organized, and to Chris Ferebee for your vision and partnership. Thanks to Vicki Crumpton for your patience and skill, and to everyone at Baker for your commitment to excellence. June Ford's keen eye focused these words—many thanks to her. Thanks to Central Christian Church for the joy of serving with you. And, thanks to Jesus, my hope, the One who knows me completely and loves me anyway. I am forever grateful.

# INTRODUCTION

*The believer is not set at the high noon of life, but at the
dawn of a new day at the point where night and day, things
passing and things to come, grapple with each other.*[1]

JÜRGEN MOLTMANN

D ad, what are you doin' here?"
      The question had rolled off my two-year-old's lips
about every thirty seconds for the past week. This particular morning, as we stood in the ticket line at the airport, I
could answer only, "I don't know." I felt disappointed.

I had looked forward to this vacation for weeks. Just the
thought of escaping e-mail, cell phones, smog, and traffic
for a few days made my heart leap. I couldn't wait to be
free from reports of gang violence, child kidnapping, and
car chases.

We had planned for this trip. We bought more supplies
than we could ever use—sunblock, travel-size shampoo,

13

soap and lotion, plenty of diapers, wipes, snack foods, and batteries for my alarm clock. We made our reservations and packed our luggage. Everything was set.

The morning of our departure the alarm went off promptly at 4:00 A.M. Quickly I got ready, woke up the family, and began to load the car. This was no small task. We had only one child at the time, but we packed enough suitcases to fill a small U-Haul truck. Our suitcases were the ones they put stickers on that say, "Caution: Over 50 Pounds."

Once we got the car loaded, the kid dressed, and the house details wrapped up, we headed to the airport. Along the way I asked, "Who is taking care of our mail?" Suddenly all the oxygen was sucked out of the car as my wife gasped. I whipped the car around and headed to a friend's house where we could leave our mailbox key under the doormat.

Back on the freeway, we were running late. My daughter was hungry. My wife was tired. And I was irritated. Only in Southern California do you hit stop-and-go traffic *before* 5:15 A.M.

When we finally got in line at the airport, we began another waiting process. Emma asked again, "Dad, what are you doin' here?" And the thought crossed my mind: *We're paying a substantial amount of money to endure this. I voluntarily put my family in this situation. It seemed like such a good idea a couple of weeks ago.*

Finally, when we got on the plane, our lovely child began to kick the seat of the elderly man in front of her. After all, she was only two. No matter how many times we told her to stop, she kept doing it. In a stroke of fatherly genius, I announced that she could watch *Snow White* on my laptop. She exploded with joy. There was only one problem: My laptop battery was dead. But I had a backup battery . . . which also turned out to be dead. *I am a loser father,* I thought. *I've ruined my child's vacation.* After a long layover and every other travel challenge imaginable, we arrived at our destination. By then we were so exhausted we just wanted to curl up and sleep. I'm not sure what we expected from our destination, but we were disappointed. We returned from our vacation twice as exhausted as when we left, almost looking forward to getting back into the daily grind.

Have you ever been so busy and distracted on a journey that, when you finally arrived at your destination, you just wanted to go home? Have you ever found that the destination just wasn't what it was cracked up to be? Unfortunately this scenario applies to too much of life. We walk across the stage at graduation and expect a diploma to come with a lifetime supply of fulfillment. We walk down the aisle, say "I do," and expect marriage to end our disagreements. We walk into a car dealership, sign on the dotted line, and expect the new car to deliver happiness. Perhaps this is why many people in all walks of life feel hopeless.

*Good Morning America* examined the struggle of hopelessness. Coanchor Diane Sawyer began the show by saying, "We are talking today about a revolution that a number of psychologists are trying to create. They believe that America is ready for a revolution of happiness because, according to statistics, there is a ten times increase in depression among kids and a ten times increase in depression among adults since the 1950s. So the question becomes, Are we doing the wrong thing? Something is not working. What do we do differently?"[2]

How do we face the explosion of depression and hopelessness? *Good Morning America*'s anchors talked about the benefit of sports. They shared stories about the power of engaging in something we love to do. They mentioned the therapeutic nature of laughter and funny movies. They quoted the remedy of Norman Cousins, a magazine editor who faced a severe form of arthritis: "Ten minutes of genuine belly laughter every day." One doctor on the show claimed he could vaccinate against unhappiness!

Despite all of the advice given on the show, the experts missed the boat. It is not that their suggestions were wrong, but they weren't enough. When the show concluded, I had the same question as when it began: Something is not working. What do we do differently?

One thing we can do is reexamine biblical hope. A major cause of Christians' hopelessness is our misunderstanding of biblical hope as merely a promise of some future event, rather than a tangible gift that can permeate, influence, and inform every aspect of our present lives. Hope is about *today, now,* transformation in *the present.*

Peter writes: "What a God we have! And how fortunate we are to have him, this Father of our Master Jesus! Because Jesus was raised from the dead, we've been given a brand-new life and have everything to live for, including a future in heaven—and the future starts now! . . . I know how great this makes you feel, even though you have to put up with every kind of aggravation in the meantime" (1 Peter 1:3–4, 6 Message).

Peter speaks of heaven's hope in terms of its daily impact. Hope transforms us at every level, including the emotive level. It makes us *feel* great, even though we face difficult circumstances. Yet today we've lost the reality of Peter's message. We think that hope's benefits come when we die, rather than when we believe. We talk about heaven as a great destination, instead of a journey we begin when we surrender to Christ. Our hope of eternity is seen as something that starts in the future, not *now*.

Our lifestyles confirm that we tend to disconnect the future from the present. In reality there is little difference in the way Christians and non-Christians live. Experts offer many reasons for this, but our lack of true future orientation is a central one. The more we live with an awareness of the future, the more holy we become in the present. Our relationships take on deeper significance, our marriages experience renewed emphasis, our goals are challenged and reoriented. Hope shifts our lives' targets and alters our current trajectories. As C. S. Lewis wrote, "Aim at heaven and you will get earth 'thrown in': aim at earth and you will get neither."[3]

*Hope That Goes the Distance* is the final book in a series on the well-known triad of the Christian life—faith, hope, and love. *Faith That Goes the Distance* explored the "hall of faith" in Hebrews 11, showing how everyday people can live extraordinary lives through faith's transforming power. *Love That Goes the Distance* examined the encouragement and practical help Jesus' love brings to the hurting. Now, *Hope That Goes the Distance* reveals how biblical hope can radically and positively influence our day-to-day lives.

Hope stands on two pillars—the character of God and the promises of God. In the following pages, we start at the beginning, with God and his character. Chapter 2 turns to the end—heaven and Revelation. Standing on God's character and his promises, the power of hope unfolds in chapters 3–8.

So, let me return to my child's question: "What are you doin' here?"

Throughout this book, we'll explore our purpose and our hope. In the process we'll learn to enjoy the journey and to hold this life loosely. We'll learn that problems, challenges, and difficulties don't have to steal our hope or our joy. We'll learn to live as though we really believe this world is not our home, because heaven will be a destination that will live up to its travel brochure.

# ONE

# A HOPE THAT TRUSTS GOD'S CHARACTER

*We have an enemy inside of us who tries to convince us that there is something out there that is better than what God wants for us, but that's not true. Every day I remind myself that what God is providing is always the best thing for me.*[1]

LAURYN HILL

A fifty-fifty chance sounds like pretty good odds. Those odds at winning the lottery are incredible. At the Super Bowl they mean you have a great shot at being the best team in the league. But a fifty-fifty chance of surviving surgery, well, that's another story. And those were the odds given Jen Powell.

Art and Jen Powell were an ordinary couple. They were the proud parents of two young children. Both worked hard and often volunteered in the community.

On March 3, 2002, Jen suddenly couldn't catch her breath. She thought she might be developing asthma and planned to visit a doctor soon. By that evening she was in the emergency room with doctors rushing around her. Her condition was serious and she was scared. A life-threatening procedure was done to reduce massive blood clots in both lungs. The doctors said they did not understand how she had survived.

During the next few months Jen returned to the hospital three more times. Doctors were unable to explain why blood thinners were not working. Eventually, after meeting with many specialists, Jen was diagnosed with a genetic blood-clotting disorder.

To ensure her survival, she took blood-thinning medication, the large doses of which threatened to eat through her stomach. If nothing changed, she would die of the genetic disorder. The doctors recommended surgery, but she faced a 50 percent chance that her blood would clot, leading to her death. Such odds are especially tough for a young couple with two young children.

I first met Art and Jen when they stopped by my church office. After a wonderful conversation, they asked their primary question: "Is it a lack of faith in God's healing ability to prepare for the possibility of death?"

I responded with a resounding no. "Even though we walk in faith," I explained, "we also use wisdom and plan appropriately. We can't use faith as an excuse to not face reality head-on."

Their questions continued. "Is it okay to video some comments to my children for them to watch in the future?" Jen asked.

"Absolutely," I said.

We shared about God's character and the importance of placing trust in him. "Are you afraid?" I asked.

"Yes," they replied, "but we are not without hope."

"We are at peace with this," Art said. "We are hopeful that God will answer our prayers in such a way that Jen will live. But if she does not, we will accept this and trust him."

Art and Jen prepared for the worst. They sold their house and downscaled.

Jen explained, "I had to focus and accept that my kids are God's. My husband is his. My life is his. I had to believe Romans 8:28, not just memorize it."

For her kids she filled a bin with items that she hoped would sustain them if she were no longer with them. Lovingly she wrote poems for her children. She explained how much she loved them, how she would miss them, and how she longed for them to place their faith in God. She wrote about how desperately she wanted to be a presence in their lives and agonized over the thought of not being there to hold them when they hurt or tuck them into bed at night. She longed to be there when they needed advice, when they were confused, when they just needed Mom to listen. She feared missing so many firsts: first report cards, first dates, first proms, first cars. She added a video of herself along with family albums she created. She wrote out cards for big occasions to come (weddings, babies, and so on). And she added prayer cards for her children. Her message to them was twofold: "I love you with all of me. I pray you will know and love Jesus Christ with all of you—your heart, soul, strength, and mind." Around her children she remained strong and positive. In private she wept at the thought of not being part of their future.

21

Four days before her surgery, Art and Jen asked me to meet with them. This time we talked about what her funeral could look like. "If I go to be with God, I want the service to be a celebration of God and his grace. I want people to know that this illness has been a gift. God has used it to strengthen our relationship with him, each other, and our children. He reminds us that each day is a gift. I want to live, but if God takes me home, I don't want the service to be all gloom. I want a celebration," Jen said.

I was astonished at their joy. How could someone have joy when facing such terrifying odds? How could they possess peace amid such a storm?

## Fear and Hope

Art and Jen discovered the power of hope based in God's character. They completely entrusted themselves to him. They rested in his will and his purpose. Paul commands: "Be joyful in hope" (Rom. 12:12). Art and Jen lived this command out in real time.

The Bible lists more than 150 references to hope. God is called the "God of hope," and Paul prays that he will "fill you with all joy and peace as you trust in him, so that you may overflow with hope by the power of the Holy Spirit" (Rom. 15:13). Any discussion of hope must start with God:

If God is not good, his promises are unreliable.

If God is not merciful, our past leaves the future in question.

If God is not sovereign, tomorrow is unsecured.

If God changes, we are potential victims of his whims.

"In the beginning God . . ." (Gen. 1:1) holds true for any discussion of hope. Most spiritual and theological problems result from a fundamental misunderstanding of God's character. As John Piper said:

> My hope as a desperate sinner, who lives in a Death Valley desert of unrighteousness, hangs on this biblical truth: that God is the kind of God who will be pleased with the one thing I have to offer—my thirst. That is why the sovereign freedom and self-sufficiency of God are so precious to me: They are the foundation of my hope that God is delighted not by the resourcefulness of bucket brigades, but by the bending down of broken sinners to drink at the fountain of grace. . . . A lifelong hope in the overflowing grace of God to meet all our needs . . . simply will not stand without a deep foundation in the doctrine of God.[2]

Both Art and Jen staked their lives on God's character and allowed it to change how they viewed the future. Human health and happiness are inevitably connected with one's view of the future. The way we see our future is more important than the way we see our present or our past. Psychologist Dr. Harold G. Wolf wrote: "Hope, like faith and a purpose in life, is medicinal. This is not merely a statement of belief but a conclusion proved by meticulously controlled scientific experiments."[3] Jen rested in this hope.

A few days before her surgery, Jen shared this poem with me:

> My trust is in Him. His master plan.
> Not for me to understand.
> If God decides I'll leave this earth,
> Don't be sad. Celebrate a birth.

I'm going to an awesome place.
Finally, I'll see His loving face.

My trust is in Him. His Master plan.
Not for me to understand.
If God decides I'll stay,
May I live my life His way.
I pray I will give Him the glory.
He is the center of my story.

His comfort and peace flood our lives.
Joy in my roles as servant, mom and wife.
You see . . . His desire for me is great.
Better than any of my plans, dreams or fate.
His love and kindness can't be measured.
He wants more for us than we can treasure.

My trust is in Him. His master plan.
Not for me to understand.

Jen said her good-byes and made the long journey to the hospital. Her friends gathered and prayed. Their hope was more than wishful thinking or blind optimism; with their hope in God they faced reality squarely and confidently.

## Living Hope

Wishful thinking is a feeling that somehow, in some form or fashion, things will work out. It is like when I turn on a football game and say, "I sure hope the Cowboys win today." The person who spends his last dollar on a lottery ticket has blind optimism. He says, "I am going to win this one, I feel it." Statistics show that you are more likely to fall out of bed, hit your head on the floor, and die than you are to win the big-money lottery. Blind optimism can be seen in the movie *Hope Floats* with Sandra Bullock and Harry Connick Jr. The last line of the movie says: "Beginnings are scary, endings are sad, but it is the middle that counts the most. You need to remember that when you find yourself at the beginning, just give hope a chance to float up, and it will too." There is some truth to that, but hope is more than just waiting for things to get better. Things could get worse.

In his book *Good to Great*, Jim Collins records a fascinating conversation with Admiral James "Jim" Stockdale. From 1965 to 1973 Admiral Stockdale was a prisoner of war at the "Hanoi Hilton" in Vietnam. He endured torture more than twenty times, suffering unimaginable brutality as the highest-ranking military officer in the camp. Even in captivity, he sought to confuse and throw off his captors. On release, he made history as the first three-star officer in the U.S. Navy to wear the Congressional Medal of Honor and the aviator wings.

Collins asked Admiral Stockdale how he dealt with the future's uncertainty in the prison camp. Admiral Stockdale said, "I never lost faith in the end of the story. I never doubted not only that I would get out, but also that I would prevail in the end and turn the experience into the defining event of my life, which, in retrospect, I would not trade."

They walked on in silence for a while, Admiral Stockdale limping because of the torture inflicted on his leg. Collins writes:

> Finally, after about a hundred meters of silence, I asked, "Who didn't make it out?"
> "Oh, that's easy," he said. "The optimists."
> "The optimists? I don't understand," I said, now completely confused, given what he'd said a hundred meters earlier.

"The optimists. Oh, they were the ones who said, 'We're going to be out by Christmas.' And Christmas would come, and Christmas would go. Then they'd say, 'We're going to be out by Easter.' And Easter would come, and Easter would go. And then Thanksgiving, and then it would be Christmas again. And they died of a broken heart. . . . This is a very important lesson. You must never confuse faith that you will prevail in the end—which you can never afford to lose—with the discipline to confront the most brutal facts of your current reality, whatever they might be."[4]

Biblical hope is not passive waiting, wishful thinking, or blind optimism. It confronts reality as it is, while holding on to the conviction of a better future. As Eugene Peterson wrote, "Hoping is not dreaming. It is not spinning an illusion of fantasy to protect us from our boredom or our pain. It means a confident alert expectation that God will do what he said he will do."[5]

Hope is sure and grounded. The Bible speaks of hope as an anchor that is firm and secure (Heb. 6:19) and a helmet of salvation that protects (1 Thess. 5:8). Paul says that everything written in the past, the entire Old Testament, was penned to give us hope (Rom. 15:4). Hope gives oxygen to faith and love, enabling them to persevere. Jürgen Moltmann wrote:

> Thus in the Christian life, faith has the priority, but hope the primacy. Without faith's knowledge of Christ, hope becomes a utopia and remains hanging in the air. But without hope, faith falls to pieces, becomes a faint-hearted and ultimately a dead faith. It is through faith that man finds the path of true life, but it is only hope that keeps him on that path. Thus it is that faith in Christ gives hope its assurance. Thus it is that hope gives faith in Christ its breath and leads it into life.[6]

When we are faced with life's harsh realities, our hope provides an enduring and preserving power.

## Hope's Power

As the doctors began to perform Jen Powell's surgery, she and Art placed their hope in God, trusting in his goodness. Though their lives were not perfect, they trusted God's mercy. Though the future seemed uncertain, they trusted God's certain control.

When Jen awoke from the anesthesia, we all breathed a sigh of relief. The next several days were critical because the bruising of her skin from the surgery could produce clots. We trusted, waited, and prayed.

Through nothing short of a miracle, Jen began to heal at a wonderful rate. She regained strength, her odds improved, and soon she was home. Within weeks she was back at church and resuming a normal life.

The doctors are constantly amazed by her progress. They have no medical explanation for her recovery. Continually the Powells remind the doctors that it is God's doing. Jen said, "I am walking one to four miles a day. I eat healthy. I go to bed early. I savor my devotion time at 5 A.M. when the house is quiet. I sit in the front window, watch the sunrise, and thank God for my life. I understand he is in charge and I am on his path." The days before and after the surgery, Jen virtually glowed when you talked with her. She still has that glow. God has taught her to hope in him alone, to be satisfied in him ultimately, and to be strengthened by him completely.

King David learned to hope in God and knew what it meant to be completely satisfied by God. In Psalm 23 David includes a powerful statement of hope: "Surely goodness and mercy shall follow me all the days of my life: and I will dwell in the house of the LORD for ever" (v. 6 KJV). *Follow* could be translated "chase" or "pursue" and was used in the context of battle pursuit. Once it described someone hunting. David and the Powells are "joyful in hope" because God is sovereign, good, and merciful; his goodness and mercy hunt and pursue them. Their perspective of the future remains anchored in the character of God.

Before we look at all the different aspects of hope, we must establish God's character as the anchor. Hope is founded on a basic trust in God's goodness, mercy, and control.

## God's Goodness

What does it mean to say that God is good? We have different definitions of *good*. My wife, Lori, has the *Pride and Prejudice* video set, five movies based on the novels of Jane Austen and set in Victorian England. They are full of romance, British accents, and everything else that makes a good chick flick. Lori and her friends swap them around; they have movie parties and exclaim over how *good* the films are.

If I watch these movies for ten minutes, I want to inflict bodily harm on myself. My criterion for a *good* movie includes explosions—preferably within the first couple of minutes. So my wife and I don't always see eye to eye on what makes a movie *good*.

The Bible says, "And we know that in all things God works for the good of those who love him, who have been called according to his purpose" (Rom. 8:28). But there are times I wonder if God and I are on different pages. Sometimes I struggle to see the good beyond the pain in the lives of some of my friends.

28

I think of Tom, who just purchased a special wheelchair for his three-year-old daughter. Doctors can't figure out why she constantly has seizures and is not developing mentally.

Then there is Susan, who has struggled through a divorce and is watching the toll it takes on her children; and Tony, who returned home after an argument with his wife to find that she had hanged herself in their home. There's Dan, a DJ in L.A. He continually reaches out to others and to God in prayer. He is a committed Christ-follower. He sees a therapist and takes his medication, but still he has bouts of paralyzing anxiety attacks that deeply disable his life.

My friend Mike was admitted to the hospital because of a viral illness. He began to have complications. Serious circulation problems ensued. Every organ in his body shut down over a six-month period, yet he lived. To keep him alive the doctors amputated both his arms and his legs. Significant scarring occurred on his face. Mike has a great attitude, but he has prosthetic arms and legs, and it takes him an incredibly long time just to get dressed each morning.

Is this God's definition of working *good* in people's lives? It doesn't seem good to me. Does God's definition of good involve pain and suffering? It kind of reminds me of prescription drugs where the "good" a drug offers is countered by the side effects of pain the drug may produce. Once I heard Kyle Idleman speak on this idea and he asked if Romans 8:28 needed a side-effects label. Have you noticed the disclaimers on most prescription drug commercials? The scene opens with a beautiful couple, walking hand in hand along the beach. This new drug has brought joy and happiness into their lives. Then, in the final moments, we hear all the negative side effects. Idleman says he once heard a spoof of these commercials. It went like this:

*Voice-over:* Take two tablets every hour for joint pain.

*Authoritative quiet voice rapid-fire:* This drug may cause joint pain, nausea, leg cramps, headache or shortness of breath. You may also experience muscle aches, rapid heartbeats, impotence, and ringing in the ears. If trips to the bathroom become greater than twelve per hour, consult your doctor. You may find yourself becoming lost or vague. May cause stigmata in Ukrainians. May induce a tendency to compulsively repeat the phrase "no can do." You may feel a powerful sense of impending doom. Do not take this product if you are uneasy with lockjaw. This drug may shorten your intestines by twenty-one feet. It has been known to cause birth defects in the user retroactively. Women experience a lowering of the voice, and an increase in ankle hair. Sensations of levitation are illusory, as is the sensation of having a "phantom" third arm. Twenty minutes after taking the pill, you will have an insatiable craving to take another dose. AVOID THIS WITH ALL YOUR POWER.[7]

So, when it comes to God's goodness, where's the side-effects label?

The Bible continually declares that God is good. Even the original Saxon term for the English *God* means "the good."[8] Nahum reminds us, "The LORD is good, a refuge in times of trouble. He cares for those who trust in him" (1:7). I might not always understand *why* something happens to God's children, but I know *what* the ultimate outcome will be—goodness. God works in our lives for our ultimate good. It doesn't mean good things always happen to us, for we live in a fallen and sinful world, but God will work whatever happens for our eternal benefit. God's primary definition of goodness is that things work together for his purpose of bringing everything together under Jesus (Eph. 1:10). As Paul said, "The grace [literally the "goodness"] of God that brings salvation has appeared to all men" (Titus 2:11).

God's goodness doesn't need a side-effects label, but sin does. Sin's side effects result in the pain we see around us. God's goodness is the primary redeeming factor of our fallen world. James says, "Every good and perfect gift is from above, coming down from the Father of the heavenly lights, who does not change like shifting shadows" (James 1:17). Everything changes in our world. Our society changes, relationships change, people change, seasons change, but through it all God remains the same. God is above all. He is not whimsical. He is not tired, sassy, or grouchy. God is not emotionally unstable. He is good and loves to do good. Stephen Charnock wrote, "This is the true and genuine character of God; he is good, he is goodness, good in himself, good in his essence, good in the highest degree, possessing whatsoever is comely, excellent, desirable; the highest good, because truly goodness in any creature is a resemblance of God."[9]

God makes all things work for his glory, which is equally for our good. This implies that every atom, every particle, every occurrence and act *ultimately* work for what is best for the Christ-follower. When we sit back in eternity and see how God worked things for our good, we will be awed with reverence and joy. Christ is managing the entire universe—every sunrise, every sunset, every flower's bloom, every ocean tide. We can trust in his care.

## A Greater Perspective

As a father, I know there are certain things that are good for my daughter, though she disagrees. Each night, as millions of Americans leisurely wrap up their evening, we at the Wilhite household have the "toothbrush drama."

As soon as I bring out the toothbrush, Emma says, "No, Daddy, I don't want it." She clenches her teeth.

"Open your mouth," I command. She laughs.

"This is not funny," I threaten. More laughter.

"If you don't open your mouth, I will put you in time-out."

Finally, I pry her mouth open. At this point, her laughter is now a halfhearted cry. She continues to resist but finally lets me brush her teeth. She may think the toothbrush is a terrible thing, but I know it is good.

God sees the eternal perspective. He is working all things for good even when we can't see it and we don't understand it. A fascinating passage about God's commitment of goodness is found in Jeremiah. He writes:

> They will be my people, and I will be their God. I will give them singleness of heart and action, so that they will always fear me for their own good and the good of their children after them. I will make an everlasting covenant with them: I will never stop doing good to them, and I will inspire them to fear me, so that they will never turn away from me. I will rejoice in doing them good and will assuredly plant them in this land with all my heart and soul.
>
> JEREMIAH 32:38–41

God was speaking to the Israelites, but he was also speaking of the everlasting agreement we now experience. These words hold true for us. He works for our good and that of our children. He will "never stop doing good." God loves to do good things for his people. He thrills to shower spiritual blessings on us. He rejoices with sheer enthusiasm and delight in doing good.

God delights in his own goodness. He takes joy in his glory and fame. Even though his happiness is complete, he rejoices in showing his goodness to make his children happy. He loves to give his goodness to others. Isaiah writes: "As a bridegroom rejoices over his bride, so will your God rejoice over you" (Isa. 62:5). God rejoices over us—he sings songs over us. What an incredible God we serve! How amazing that he is filled with passion for our good! How awe inspiring that we are the focus of his pleasure! How humbling that we are the objects of his grace! Our hope is anchored in his goodness and mercy.

## God's Mercy

Did you ever play "uncle" growing up? We always called it "mercy." I remember being pinned to the floor as a friend bent my arm in inhuman directions. "Say mercy and I'll stop," he said. I held off until the very last resource drained from my body and then uttered the word of humiliation and defeat, "Mercy." Saying "mercy" was acceptable when several kids dog piled you and put you in a near-death headlock. There was respect in getting up with dirt all over you, a warrior hopelessly outnumbered. But when a kid grabbed your pinky finger and bent it back, you felt totally awkward and wimpy to yelp for mercy. Playground mercy meant stopping the pain.

David looked to the future and realized that because he served a merciful God, mercy would pursue him all the days of his life. God's mercy is so much more than a playground game. David wrote, "The LORD is gracious, and full of compassion; slow to anger, and of great mercy" (Ps. 145:8 KJV). God is described as being "rich in mercy" (Eph. 2:4).

Mercy is the extension of God's goodness in stooping to help needy sinners. God's mercy is seen all through the Bible. When Adam and Eve took the first bite of the apple and were allowed another breath—mercy. When the Israelites set up and worshiped idols, God took them back—mercy. When Abraham lied or Moses committed murder or David committed adultery, and God didn't strike them down—mercy. Through the prophets God mourns the fact that people have rejected his mercy. Even in God's judgment, we often see him yearning to pour out his mercy. "Who is a God like you," asks Micah, "who pardons sin and forgives the transgression of the remnant of his inheritance? You do not stay angry forever but delight to show mercy" (Micah 7:18). God delights in showing mercy!

God cares how we see our future. What do you see in yours? We learn much about ourselves when we explore this, because our personality influences our view of the future.

To people pleasers, nothing is ever good enough. A people pleaser could write a best-selling book, and it would not be good enough. People pleasers have a tendency to see flaws, not mercy, in the future.

Compulsive people may fear their own bad habits and see roadblocks to mercy, rather than God's mercy, in the future. The psalmist says that God takes "pleasure in them that fear him, in those that hope in his mercy" (Ps. 147:11 KJV). In the future we will fail, sin, make mistakes, say things we regret, experience pain and suffering, but God delights when we revere him and put our hope in his mercy. So Peter directs us: "Set your hope fully on the grace to be given you when Jesus Christ is revealed" (1 Peter 1:13). *Set* implies a decisive action, which is intensified by the adverb *fully*, meaning "firmly." Biblical realism gives us a perspective of the future that should fill us with joy.

How can we be sure of God's future mercy? God guaranteed his mercy by promise and oath. Hebrews reminds us of God's promise to Abraham and, as followers of Christ, to us. Hebrews says:

> Because God wanted to make the unchanging nature of his purpose very clear to the heirs of what was promised, he confirmed it with an oath. God did this so that, by two unchangeable things in which it is impossible for God to lie, we who have fled to take hold of the hope offered to us may be greatly encouraged. We have this hope as an anchor for the soul, firm and secure.
>
> HEBREWS 6:17–19

God can swear by no one greater than himself. This eternal God who is all-powerful and all-knowing, who owes us absolutely nothing, bound himself to us by swearing by himself. His mercy and promise are guaranteed, based on his character and faithfulness to himself.

This is our grounding anchor in the storms of life—Jesus, our hope (1 Tim. 1:1). He is the anchor of mercy that keeps us from drifting and drowning. He is our security, righteousness, wisdom, and joy.

## A New Beginning

Dietrich Bonhoeffer, the renowned German theologian, writer, and thinker, found hope in God's character and promise. As Hitler rose to power and began to dominate much of Europe, Bonhoeffer wrestled with his ethical responsibilities as a Christian. He had spoken out against Hitler for years, but he could see the inhumane treatment of Jews and others moving to new levels. He began to reason this way: If you see a car about to plow into a group of innocent people and kill them, and you have the opportunity to grab the steering wheel to avert the disaster, what do you do? If you do nothing, you are guilty of the death of innocent people. If you grab the wheel, you are guilty of injuring or killing the people in the car. Which is the worse evil?

Bonhoeffer chose to grab the wheel. He worked to undermine Hitler's regime and was involved in a conspiracy to assassinate the dictator. On March 12, 1943, a briefcase with explosives was smuggled onto a plane on which Hitler was traveling, but fuses malfunctioned and the plane reached its destination safely. A week later, Major von Gersdorff was to meet with Hitler. A bomb was in his briefcase, but Hitler cut the meeting short after only ten minutes. On another occasion the conspirators waited in vain for a code word in Berlin so they could begin an uprising. It never came. This was one of many assassination attempts they plotted. None of them succeeded.

On April 5, 1943, Bonhoeffer was arrested for his activities and he remained in jail for two years. His letters from this period were later published as *Letters and Papers from Prison* and they give us a powerful vision of his experience and his faith. On Sunday, April 8, 1945, Bonhoeffer held a service in one of the prison camps. He spoke on the text: "Praise be to the God and Father of our Lord Jesus Christ! In his great mercy he has given us new birth into a living hope. . . ." (1 Peter 1:3). After the message the guards came and said, "Prisoner Bonhoeffer, get ready and come with us." He knew what that meant.

On the morning of April 9, 1945, Bonhoeffer prayed and then with quiet resolve went to the gallows where he was hanged. His body was tossed among the hundreds of corpses and burned. His last words were intended for his friend George Bell: "This is the end; for me it is the beginning of life. I believe in universal Christian brotherhood which rises above national interests and I believe that our victory is certain."[10] One month later the Allied forces secured the victory and World War II came to an end.

We can argue about Bonhoeffer's actions—something that is easy to do when we don't have to live through his experiences—but there is no argument about his perspective: "This is the end; for me it is the beginning." He looked forward to that "city with foundations, whose architect and builder is God" (Heb. 11:10). Even in the midst of suffering, there was hope. He trusted the character of God and held on to the reality of reward and eternal life. It is to this reality—heaven—we now turn our attention.

**Questions for Discussion**

1. What are some things in which people put their hope?
2. What is the difference between blind optimism and biblical hope?
3. Romans 8:28 reads: "And we know that in all things God works for the good of those who love him, who have been called according to his purpose." Does this imply bad things will never happen to a Christian?
4. How can we expect God to work for our good?
5. What are some ways God reveals his mercy to you?
6. How do God's goodness and mercy help you view the future with hope?

# TWO

# A Hope That Is Stored in Heaven

*There have been times when I think we do not desire heaven, but more often I find myself wondering whether, in our heart of hearts, we have ever wanted anything else.*[1]

C. S. Lewis

Janet sat on the shower floor and screamed angrily at God. In the middle of the night she cried until her pillow was wet. Some days she couldn't stop crying. The thoughts that crossed her mind made her feel guilty. Life's demands had drained her every resource. Daily chores appeared impossible. Energy gave way to apathy. Resolve gave way to fatigue. She had reached her limit, the darkest valley of her life, a valley from which many do not emerge.

Six years earlier Janet's life had changed forever. After a difficult pregnancy, during which she spent six months in bed, she gave birth to a daughter she and her husband named Dana. The baby was six weeks premature. Complications arose from the moment of Dana's birth. Within two weeks the diagnosis was confirmed—cerebral palsy, severe mental retardation, and blindness.

Janet listened to the prognosis in shock. The doctor continued speaking, but the questions in Janet's mind drowned out his voice. The hopes and dreams Janet and her husband, Rob, had for Dana's future faded. All the expectations were crushed: hearing Dana say "mommy" the first time, watching her take her first steps, playing with her friends. For months nothing penetrated the numbness Janet felt. Of course Rob felt equally overwhelmed with a sense of loss and grief coming in waves. Suddenly they were faced with many demanding choices—would they raise Dana in their home or place her in a facility for special-needs children? Would Janet continue to work or quit her job to care for Dana? Would they be able to afford the proper care at all? And there were spiritual questions: Where was God in all of this? How could this be happening?

After much prayer and counsel, Janet decided to stop working and began to devote herself to her new full-time job—taking care of Dana. They chose to raise Dana in their own home and, with the support of friends and family, Rob and Janet played the cards they were dealt. Loving Dana completely and unselfishly, they became models as parents of special-needs children. They researched books and learned how to care for their daughter. Janet leaned on

God and turned to her journal where she recorded thoughts and prayers.

Taking care of Dana remained a daunting task. At six years old, Dana could not sit unsupported or roll over from front to back. She could not walk or speak and could communicate only yes and no. She had no functional use of her hands and needed to be fed and cared for in every way. She could see only shadows. Often she woke in the night needing help. This, coupled with continual trips to therapists, doctors, and hospitals, was extremely stressful. Still Rob and Janet had wonderful times with Dana. They chose to enjoy life, laugh together, and make room for fun. They refused to be victims.

Someone told Janet that after age seven Dana would show no progress. Even though doctors assured her this was not the case, Janet began having a breakdown as Dana neared her seventh birthday. She wrote in her journal:

This last year has been a year of looking back and reassessing Dana's progress. Some of the conclusions I have made are:

- She is six years old and still doesn't seem to like to do much other than suck on her fingers.
- I still have to go down the infant aisle in the toy store to find her anything to play with.
- Physical therapy has made no progress in two years and is strictly maintenance at this point.
- Occupational therapy at 7:30 in the morning twenty miles away is a pain in the neck, and the therapist has admitted that she doesn't think that Dana will ever be feeding herself; although, that is what she is still working on!
- I'm having a hard time getting over the hump into acceptance; I am realizing that maybe I am upset about this

because I really don't accept Dana fully for what she is and who she is right now. I want more.[2]

Imagine the difficulty of accepting that your child will never run and play, never date, never ask your advice. Consider the despair in believing you have done all you can do but it's not enough. To top it off, Janet struggled with such questions as: Should I be the miracle mom who works for ten long years so that her daughter can grasp a peg for five seconds? Is it worth it? Inevitably these questions would result in a sense of guilt and add to her struggle.

During this period, Dana slept uneasily. Janet felt depressed and exhausted from too many sleepless nights. Every parent has "insanity" moments under much less stress. Janet says, "One night when I was especially exhausted, I heard Dana crying again and I imagined that she was laughing at me. Everything inside of me was longing to get up out of bed, go to her room, and hold a pillow over her face until she stopped breathing. Thus I would be putting both of us out of our misery. I began to sob terribly with guilt. How could I ever think I was a good mother if I could allow myself to contemplate killing my child? *I must be the most terrible person in the world,* I told myself."[3]

As Janet wrestled with this, she hit bottom. Thankfully, at her personal bottom, God's strong arms brought hope and encouragement. Janet reached out and asked for help with Dana and slowly she emerged from this dark period. She says, "In facing the challenges head-on, I realized I had a choice. I could either wallow in frustration or choose to accept the promises of God. Not just the promises of heaven, but the hope that he will be there for me at any moment day or night when I need strength.

Hope means that God is with me and beside me. He will sustain me. That gets me through when I am frustrated or scared."[4]

Janet arrived at a place of acceptance for Dana. Yet Janet is not content with Dana's condition. There is a difference. She is not content that Dana struggles just to reach out and touch something. Nor is she content that Dana gets frustrated when she can't communicate. But she accepts her unconditionally and lives with the hope that one day she will be whole and able to do everything in heaven. That hope is a tangible reality. Caring for Dana reminds her of the brokenness of our world, but it also inspires her to live with her sights on what is to come.

Through the years her hope has carried her the distance. With great assurance she believes that this life is not the end. By the time Dana reached age fifteen, Rob and Janet had become fulfilled parents. Janet asserts, "We live with so much hope that if God were to take Dana tomorrow, I would be very sad, but I would also know she is in another place and she is finally at peace and in comfort. She is in God's arms. She will have the new body she has been waiting for."[5] For Rob, Janet, and Dana, heaven is not a simple pipe dream but a present reality that gives them sustaining power to face daily challenges.

## What Dreams May Come

In *What Dreams May Come*, Chris Nielsen, played by Robin Williams, dies and finds himself in heaven. There he asks Albert, played by Cuba Gooding Jr., "Where is God in all this?" Albert responds, "He's up there, somewhere, shouting down that he loves us, wondering why we can't hear him. . . ."

That is a far cry from the biblical descriptions of heaven where we will see God's face and his name will be on our foreheads!

Our culture has become fascinated with heaven. On television there are shows that highlight the afterlife, and movies seek to reassure us that death is not to be feared. But Hollywood's conception of life after death bears little resemblance to the biblical one. *Time* presented the topic in its cover story, "Does Heaven Exist?" The article claimed:

> Heaven is AWOL. This is not to say that Americans think death ends everything or even that they doubt heaven's existence. People still believe in it; it's just that their concept of exactly what it is has grown foggier, and they hear about it much less frequently from their pastors. To reverse the words of the old spiritual: Everybody's goin' to heaven, just ain't talkin' 'bout it. The silence is such that it sometimes seems heaven might as well not be there.[6]

As our culture latches on to the concept of heaven and wrestles with it, the church is too often silent.

*Time* asked participants, "Do you believe in the existence of heaven where people live forever with God after they die?" Eighty-one percent of the people responded yes; 13 percent responded no.[7] Despite an overwhelming belief in heaven, our questions persist: What happens when we die? Where do we go?

When it comes to the afterlife, the only reliable source of information for Christians is the Bible, which gives us glimpses from God's perspective. The Bible teaches us that heaven is a marvelous place, a place of eternal bliss. While we don't know all there is to know about heaven (God has not revealed heaven fully), it is important for us to contemplate the things that are clear in Scripture. Contrary to *What*

*Dreams May Come*, heaven is not simply whatever we imagine it to be for ourselves. God is preparing a specific place for us, and we will see that it is an essential part of our hope.

## A Glorious Body

Heaven holds out the hope of a new body. When we roll out of bed in the morning and stand to feel the ache of a twenty-year-old ankle injury, or when the arthritis flares up again, we long for a new body. Paul's heart was so fixed on this hope he groaned, "longing to be clothed with our heavenly dwelling" (2 Cor. 5:2).

For Janet Morel the hope of a new body allows her to stand proudly with her daughter. In public with Dana, Janet faces embarrassment from others' constant stares. Rather than flinching or hiding, Janet stands tall. She has great self-esteem and knows that no matter what anyone says, she and Dana are special in God's eyes. And the Morels have a hope that in heaven Dana will be free to run and play. The hope of Dana's new body allows them to face each morning.

What is this new body going to be like that Dana and all believers will experience in heaven? Will we be like ghosts—mists that float around and interact with other mists? The Bible hints that our new bodies will be our earthly bodies, glorified. The bodies we receive in the resurrection will have the same qualities as the glorified resurrection body of Christ.

After the resurrection, Jesus' body had many of the characteristics of his earthly body. His scars were visible. He could be examined and touched. He ate breakfast with Peter and walked the Emmaus road with two disciples. His physical body was real.

His body also had supernatural qualities. For instance, he moved through solid walls and would periodically appear in such a way that his identity was not immediately apparent. Paul writes, "But our citizenship is in heaven. And we eagerly await a Savior from there, the Lord Jesus Christ, who, by the power that enables him to bring everything under his control, will transform our lowly bodies so that they will be like his glorious body" (Phil. 3:20–21). Our new bodies will be ours, but they will be perfect. The good news is that they will be without pain. For years my mother suffered from chronic back pain. Then a while ago she stepped out of a motor home and missed the last step. When her foot hit the ground, her hip was jammed up into her back. She thought, *I'll never walk again.*

But that night in bed she said to my father, "I don't feel any pain."

My dad sat up and said, "Well, can you wiggle your toes?" Like, are you still alive? Is everything functioning? They checked the vital signs. She was still breathing and without pain. She ended up going weeks with no pain and months with improved pain—all from a mishap. That is only a fleeting glimpse of what is to come in heaven.

Some of you live with pain every day, but a day is coming when your body and mind will be completely pain free. Heaven will be free from disease, death, X-rays, test results, and suffering. There will be no radiation, no chemotherapy, no waiting for the doctor, no dentures, no counting fat grams, no eyeglasses, no hearing aids, no wheelchairs, no artificial limbs, no arthritis. New bodies! What an incredible hope!

Perspective changes everything, especially the perspective that some day we will receive a new body. Though here on earth we are slowly wasting away in our physical bodies, a day is coming when we will receive eternal bodies to go with our eternal home.

## A Big, Big House

I have a love/hate relationship with our local Tour of Homes. Each year we take the tour to look at all the incredible new houses. As we pile in the car to make the trip, I think about how much I love our house. Gratitude fills my heart that we have a place to live. Then we take the tour. The ceilings in the new homes always seem higher, the trim more ornate, the atmosphere more enticing. After several hours of traipsing through these beautiful houses, we return to our home. Pulling into our driveway, I look up and suddenly my "castle" is a "shack." My gratitude is replaced with "If our house only had this . . . if only it had that. . . ." It's been several months since the Tour of Homes, so I am once again in love with our home.

The Bible teaches that someday there will be a new heaven and a new earth that will be a million times better than anything on the Tour of Homes. Peter tells us, "But the day of the LORD will come like a thief. The heavens will disappear with a roar; the elements will be destroyed by fire, and the earth and everything in it will be laid bare" (2 Peter 3:10). But there will be a new heaven and a new earth.

The original language used to describe the new earth indicates it is not only new, it is also different. The new heaven and earth will be glorified, never ending, and free from sin and death. The Bible does not give us all the specifics on what the new heaven and earth will look like, but it will have similarities to earth. We read of the city of Jerusalem being there, though substantially bigger. The new Jerusalem is described with terms that remind us of any city: walls, gates, streets. In the book of Revelation we read of a high mountain, water, a stream, and trees. Revelation 21 is the most descriptive passage in the Bible about our new home—the new Jerusalem. John writes:

> Then I saw a new heaven and a new earth, for the first heaven and the first earth had passed away, and there was no longer any sea. I saw the Holy City, the new Jerusalem, coming down out of heaven from God, prepared as a bride beautifully dressed for her husband.
>
> And I heard a loud voice from the throne saying, "Now the dwelling of God is with men, and he will live with them. They will be his people, and God himself will be with them and be their God. He will wipe every tear from their eyes. There will be no more death or mourning or crying or pain, for the old order of things has passed away."
>
> He who was seated on the throne said, "I am making everything new!"
>
> REVELATION 21:1–5

The city originates in heaven and comes down. One of the first things John says is that there is no sea. Water covers most of the current earth and for the ancients it symbolized boundaries and fear. In heaven there will be neither. The only water described in heaven is "a pure river of water of life, clear as crystal, proceeding out of the throne of God and of the Lamb" (Rev. 22:1 KJV). The river flows right down heaven's main street.

The dimensions of the new Jerusalem are given as a cube: "The city was laid out like a square, as long as it was wide. He measured the city with the rod and found it to be 12,000 stadia in length, and as wide and high as it is long" (21:16).

John's 12,000 stadia equals 1,500 miles. It is hard to imagine 1,500 miles in height. On the current earth, 1,500 miles extends well out of the earth's atmosphere, which is only 100 miles deep. Are these measurements symbolic? Perhaps, but I tend to think not, because John says, "He measured its wall and it was 144 cubits thick, by man's measurement, which the angel was using" (21:17). It seems that God is trying to tell us something very descriptive and clear. The angel is measuring "by man's measurement."

If that is the case, then as John MacArthur writes, "According to these measurements, the New Jerusalem covers a surface area of 2.25 million square miles. By comparison, all of greater London is six-hundred-and-twenty-one square miles. . . . On that basis, the New Jerusalem would be able to house over eleven billion people and that is not taking into account the incredible height of the city!"[8]

Fifteen hundred miles is about the distance from Maine to Florida. Imagine such an area squared off, then cubed. It is enormous in size and proportion with intersecting levels of golden streets. What an overwhelming mental picture![9]

One person said, "The good news to me about heaven is that it is not bid out to the lowest bidder." God has spared no expense in creating this eternal home. It will be spectacular. Don't fear that you'll be lost in a crowded, noisy, polluted city. Remember that our new bodies won't be subject to the same limitations as they are now. Likely travel won't be a problem. And I imagine God has a pretty effective public works department. Heaven will make everything human pale in comparison.

One way to explain the unexplainable to people is to tell them what something is not. I have a friend on the mission field who said he struggled with explaining things in America like grocery stores and heaters. The tribal peoples he worked with did not get it. So he resorted to telling them what America is not. "In America we do not go hungry; we do not have to travel to get water; our homes are not hot in the summer or cold in the winter." In the Bible we get glimpses of heaven, but primarily it tells us what heaven won't be. "There will be no more death or mourning or crying or pain, for the old order of things has passed away" (Rev. 21:4).

I read of one of the most expensive houses in Britain being put on the market for fifty-six million U.S. dollars. Number 15a Kensington Palace Gardens is twenty thousand square feet. The interior is decorated with silk curtains, marble floors, and antique mirrors. Its three stories contain ten bedrooms, nine bathrooms, staff quarters, and an industrial-size kitchen connected to a huge dining room. The master bedroom is connected by an elevator to the house's most incredible feature: a swimming pool built in an orangery. The house also has its own steam room and gymnasium. But compared to what we read in Revelation one word comes to my mind: shack. A day is coming when we will walk on streets of gold.

**Take This Job and Love It!**

I'll never forget working the morning shift at Grandy's restaurant. I had to arrive at work by 5:30 each morning. My first job: make the gravy. Now, the gravy was art, and there was time for only one shot at making it. If you got it wrong, the gravy was messed up for the entire day. I know. I got it wrong. I would have learned more quickly if my supervisor hadn't been a gravy taskmaster! Every morning she barked out the gravy details to me.

Another thing I learned at Grandy's was how to crack eggs in all kinds of creative ways—on my forehead, elbow, knee, and on any kind of inanimate object. I could even do the ultimate—crack two eggs on each other and empty the yolks together into the pan with no shell! Aren't you impressed? This was the highlight of my work in those days.

It has been estimated that there are more than fifty thousand occupations in the United States. Yet how many people do you know who are truly satisfied with their work? There are personnel problems, lack of adequate pay, long hours, overbearing bosses, and monotonous tasks. Continually people find themselves doing things they do not enjoy. But in heaven those problems will all be behind us.

Heaven won't be a place of inactivity or boredom. It is not, as one Sunday school student once thought, an eternally long worship service where we will begin in the hymn book singing page one and continue until we've sung all the way through. We will have productive work to do.

One of the things we will do in heaven is worship. Don't associate this with boring. The idea of singing forever in a choir robe would not cause me to look forward to heaven. I actually had a choir teacher tell me to lip-synch on a choir tour! But the reality of heaven is quite different. And our worship will be filled with passion.

Not only will we worship, we will also serve. I am not sure what this service will entail, but we will have duties. And we will experience happiness and fulfillment in our occupations! If you feel you've missed fulfillment in your job here, be assured—you won't miss it in heaven.

## The Big Picture

We live in a fallen world filled with pain and difficulty. Children are born with disabilities, others are homeless, and some are abused. Families fall apart, and crime runs rampant. The suffering of our world is evidence that when Adam and Eve ate the fruit in the Garden of Eden, more than innocence was lost. Yet God is not finished with us.

Consider the amazing symmetry between Genesis 1–3 and Revelation 20–22, the first and last sections of the Bible. In Genesis we read about how the world got into terrible trouble, but in Revelation we get a picture of how God will restore all things to the perfection he originally intended. Look at the comparisons below and note that the realm of heaven will be free from evil and quite different from earth.[10]

| Genesis 1–3 | Revelation 20–22 |
| --- | --- |
| "In the day that you eat from it, you shall surely die" (2:17). | "There shall no longer be any death" (21:4). |
| Satan appears as deceiver (3:1). | Satan removed forever (20:10). |
| "I will greatly multiply your pain" (3:16). | "There shall no longer be any . . . pain" (21:4). |
| "Cursed is the ground because of you" (3:17). | "There shall no longer be any curse" (Rev. 22:3). |
| First paradise closed (3:23). | New paradise opened (21:25). |
| They were driven from God's presence (3:24). | "They shall see his face" (22:4). |

The place we are heading will be free from the curse, free from Satan, free from death. As a pastor I have performed my share of funerals. I can't wait for the day when I see some of those families reunited, when their tears are turned to rejoicing, when the relationships that were halted begin again. Wives will be reunited with their husbands, children with their parents. Friends and associates will rejoice in seeing each other again. There will be no more good-byes, no more abrupt endings. People who experience so much pain and loss at death's hands will rejoice in the glory of God and the joy of one another.

Once the hope of heaven is embedded in our minds, authentic joy wells up within us. Our perspective on life is altered. The apostle Paul was whipped with thirty-nine lashes on five different occasions; he was beaten with a rod three times; he was shipwrecked three times; he was nearly stoned to death; he was deprived of food and water and clothing. Yet he declares, "I consider that our present sufferings are not worth comparing with the glory that will be revealed in us" (Rom. 8:18). Again he says, "No eye has seen, no ear has heard, no mind has conceived what God has prepared for those who love him" (1 Cor. 2:9).

Think of the things in life that you consider to be wonderful and amazing: pecan pie with Blue Bell ice cream; a warm cappuccino on a cold, cloudy day; a midday ride on a Harley; the feeling of complete relaxation fifteen minutes after getting out of the hot tub. Think of the most amazing things in life and multiply those things by a million. Paul says we cannot begin to grasp what is waiting for us.

The best part of heaven is not the benefits we will receive. It will be the experience of God himself. We were created to love God and enjoy him forever. In heaven we will be overwhelmed by his majesty, beauty, and excellency. God will be "all in all" (1 Cor. 15:28). We will be enraptured as we see more of God's wonders.

Many couples feel that after several years of marriage, they have exhausted the other's love. They have expressed love in every way they know how, they have seen all there is to see in the other, and the relationship plateaus. Not so with God. For all eternity he will become more and more beautiful. We will forever learn more about him and worship him. The opportunities for showing our love to him in new ways will be endless. As Augustine said, "He shall be the end of our desires who shall be seen without end . . . praised without weariness."[11]

Jesus ate, worked, talked, and shared life with his disciples on earth, and we will have a similar fellowship with him in heaven. Jesus will be exalted to the highest degree, but exaltation will not make him inaccessible. Christ is uplifted as our representative, advocate, high priest, and bridegroom. We are exalted with him. We will be transformed into Jesus' image, with a glorious body like his. We will reign with him, inherit his riches, celebrate his goodness, and experience unhindered communion with him. As we see him exalted, we will be filled with more awe and adoration and we will desire him more passionately forever.

Our happiness on earth is fragile, but in heaven our joy will increase forever. We often think of heaven as a static state of bliss, but why wouldn't our pleasure continually increase as our understanding of God increases? Jonathan Edwards gets at this when he writes of those in heaven: "Their having perfect happiness does not exclude all increase, nor does it exclude all hope, for we do not know but they will increase in happiness for ever."[12] In many places Edwards hints at this. Even in heaven we will not fully grasp God. For us to completely understand him would be for us to be God. So for all of eternity we will learn more of his majesty, and for all of eternity we will be increasing in our happiness and joy as we do.

In heaven God's fame will be universally established and he will be glorified. All of his work in bringing the world to salvation will be complete. We will marvel at it, for the church will be beautiful, finally without blemish. We will behold how awesome God is in his strength, power, acts, and love. The feast, the wedding celebration of the Lamb, will continue for eternity. Since we will never exhaust God or his glory, we will move from glory to glory, from happiness to happiness.

Our vision of the next life is often far too limited. Heaven puts a new spin on everything. No matter how difficult our lives may be, no matter how deep the pain, it cannot be compared to the joy that awaits us. It allows people like Janet Morel to experience joy in the difficulties. She says, "I live with the full expectation that God will be there to listen and comfort. He gives me confidence in my own worth and Dana's worth, and I know I can trust him. I expect him to use us for his glory and desire for him to do so. And, until we experience the joy of heaven, I look forward to God using Dana, just as she is, to touch and bless the lives of hurting people. This is my hope."[13]

The Bible is clear. If we place our trust in Jesus, our name is written in the Lamb's book of life. A glorious new body; a big, big house; an amazing reunion; and a wonderful job will be ours!

Once, as George MacDonald talked with his son about the future, his son said, "It seems too good to be true." "Nay," MacDonald responded, "it is just so good it must be true!"[14]

## Questions for Discussion

1. Name all the movies you can think of that deal with heaven. How do these movies portray heaven? Which aspects seem biblical? Which do not?
2. What things about heaven do you look forward to the most?

3. The Bible says we will receive new bodies in the afterlife. While there is much about this we do not know, what are some characteristics we learn from the Bible about these bodies?
4. What are some similarities and differences between our current earth and the new earth?
5. What difference can the hope of heaven make in our lives now?

# THREE

# A HOPE THAT ANTICIPATES JESUS' RETURN

*For all that has been, thanks. For all that shall be, yes.*[1]

DAG HAMMARSKJÖLD

It was a hot Texas day. With each passing moment my expectations rose. At precisely six o'clock, I pulled up into Lori's driveway and made my way to the door. We smiled for a photo her parents insisted on and headed out for what she thought was a normal date. My plan, though, was to take her for a romantic meal and then walk to a park where I would ask her to marry me.

Everything was going perfectly. We arrived at the restaurant, which was on the top floor of the tallest building in our city, and sat down for dinner. During the meal, I looked out the window and saw it was raining—not a little shower but a drenching downpour. My romantic plan washed away before my eyes.

Remaining calm and cool on the outside, I desperately pieced together plan B. I had no choice but to propose in the restaurant. My only problem: The ring was in my car, several floors below. I excused myself for the restroom and took the elevator to the bottom floor. After making the mad dash to the car, I was completely soaked.

"Where have you been?" Lori asked as I sat back down at the table.

"I ran down to the car."

"Why?"

Suddenly all my romantic charm was swallowed up in one classic "guy" response: "Uh, I needed to get my nose spray." (*Nose spray!* What was I thinking?!) Fortunately she hadn't yet learned that, because I was a man, I would utter these "perfect moment" sayings all the time.

"That's funny," she said. "I have your nasal spray right here in my purse."

I was busted. *Don't make it worse,* I told myself. Instead, I took her hands in mine and quoted a passage in Ruth: "Don't urge me to leave you or to turn back from you. Where you go I will go, and where you stay I will stay. Your people will be my people and your God my God. Where you die I will die, and there I will be buried" (Ruth 1:16–17).

Then I dropped to one knee and asked, "Will you be my date for life? Will you marry me?" In that moment I heard the only word I wanted to hear: "YES!" I can't remember much else that happened. I was too awed by the realization that despite all my faults and all my character flaws, she had said yes.

Amazing grace! But it is not nearly as amazing as the yes God pronounces to us. Paul writes, "For no matter how many promises God has made, they are 'Yes' in Christ. And so through him the 'Amen' is spoken by us to the glory of God" (2 Cor. 1:20). God has already said yes! Paul does not write that *some* of the promises are yes, but *all* of them are yes in Christ—promises to give us hope and a future, promises to give us healing and strength. When we ask, "God, will you help me?" the answer is already yes in Christ. Will you forgive me, love me, and hear my cry? Yes. Will you take care of me, heal me, and guide me? Yes. Will you reveal yourself to me? Yes. Will you transform me by your spirit and soften my heart? Yes. Will you make it all worth it someday? Yes. God has made hundreds of promises and all of them are yes in Christ.

So "we wait," as Paul writes, "for the blessed hope—the glorious appearing of our great God and Savior, Jesus Christ" (Titus 2:13). We long for the day of Christ's return, when God's yes will be fulfilled. This *blessed hope,* coupled with the fact that God keeps his promises, should give us courage, perspective, and deep inner happiness in the trenches of life.

We have explored God's character and promise, but the most immediate aspect of hope involves the second coming of Jesus. Heaven is a powerful hope, but Jesus' soon return inspires obedience. It is not that the blessed hope is the *appearing* of Jesus; our blessed hope *is* Jesus. All of God's promises come to fruition in the person of Jesus. So we look forward to and long for his return.

## End-Times Mania

As we look forward to this blessed hope, we can become confused. Continually we are bombarded with different opinions and views on Jesus' return. Since the beginning of time, people have made predictions about the future. Some are quite humorous. For example:

In A.D. 100, Julius Sextus Frontinus, a Roman engineer, said: "Inventions have long since reached their limit, and I see no hope for further developments."

In 1893, journalist Junius Henri Browne claimed: "Law will be simplified [over the next century]. Lawyers will have diminished, and their fees will have been vastly curtailed."

In 1946, John von Neumann, the computer scientist, claimed: "It would appear we have reached the limits of what it is possible to achieve with computer technology."

In 1959, United States Postmaster General Arthur Summerfield claimed: "Before man reaches the moon, your mail will be delivered within hours from New York to Australia by guided missiles. We stand on the threshold of rocket mail."

In 1995, Bob Metcalfe said: "I predict the Internet . . . will go spectacularly supernova and in 1996 catastrophically collapse."[2]

People continually make predictions, but predictions are risky business. In fact *The Futurist* staff conducted a study of the predictions made in the magazine over the last thirty years. It found that the best predictors had only a 68 percent accuracy rate with twenty-three hits and eleven misses. In 1984 *The Economist* staff questioned a wide range of professionals, from CEOs to finance specialists to garbage collectors, about their predictions concerning what the economic state would be during the next ten years. Who do you think made the most accurate predictions? They found the garbage collectors and CEOs did better than the finance specialists![3] Predicting the future is risky business.

This is why it is so important that we know what Jesus said about his return. In Mark 13 Jesus sits on the Mount of Olives and talks to his friends about his second coming. He says:

> No one knows about that day or hour, not even the angels in heaven, nor the Son, but only the Father. Be on guard! Be alert! You do not know when that time will come. It's like a man going away: He leaves his house and puts his servants in charge, each with his assigned task, and tells the one at the door to keep watch.
>
> Therefore keep watch because you do not know when the owner of the house will come back—whether in the evening, or at midnight, or when the rooster crows, or at dawn. If he comes suddenly, do not let him find you sleeping. What I say to you, I say to everyone: "Watch!"
>
> MARK 13:32–37

The one thing he emphasizes is that we do not know when he will return: "No one knows about that day or hour. . . . You do not know when that time will come. . . . you do not know when the owner of the house will come back" (vv. 32, 33, 35). Despite this, there are still people out there telling us exactly when Jesus will come back.

It's understandable that, in A.D. 960 when a German theologian named Bernard of Thuringia predicted the world would end in A.D. 992, panic spread as the year approached.

Hundreds of years later people wouldn't be much smarter. In 1843 William Miller wrote: "Desolating earthquakes, sweeping fires, distressing poverty, political profligacy, private bankruptcy and widespread immorality which abound in these last days, obviously indicate that the Lord is returning immediately." Miller took fifty thousand Christians on October 22, 1844, to a mountain and they waited all night for Jesus to return. They had sold their property, thrown everything to the wind, and headed for the mountain. Some climbed trees and watched the stars and waited. On the morning of October 23, after nothing had happened, they walked back into the city amid jeering and taunting. It was a tragic day in church history.[4]

Surely by the enlightened twentieth century, we would know more. But then there is, among others, Edgar Whisenant. After September 1, 1989, Whisenant said to the press, "I can stand in front of the Lord and say I gave it my best shot." In the mid-eighties, Whisenant wrote a book—*88 Reasons Why the Rapture Will Happen in 1988*. This was his reasoning: We can't know the day or the hour, but we can know the month and the year. When it didn't happen in 1988, he came out with a sequel on why it would happen in 1989. After an 0-for-2 record in predicting when Jesus would return, the retired NASA engineer, who lived in a one-room shack outside Little Rock, Arkansas, said his job was done. His book predicting the 1989 rapture sold only thirty thousand copies in contrast to his first book, which reportedly sold more than two million.[5]

People try to predict when the end will come, but Jesus says, "No one knows." It is like a man who puts servants in charge of his house and then goes away. The man is coming back, but the servants don't know when. The only sure thing is that he will return.

## Signs That the End Is Near

In Mark 13 Jesus gives three signs that reveal the end is near.

### 1. The Temple Destroyed

As Jesus sits on the Mount of Olives, he points to the temple and says, "Do you see all these great buildings? . . . Not one stone here will be left on another; every one will be thrown down" (Mark 13:2). Forty years after Jesus died, the Romans came in and destroyed the temple (A.D. 70) under the guise of suppressing an insurrection. They took the temple completely apart—not one stone left on another, except for the foundation stones, which were not part of the main temple edifice. Josephus said that, after the Romans were finished, you could not tell any building had been there, much less one of the ancient world's most magnificent.

### 2. Persecution

The second sign Jesus gives for his return is persecution. Jesus said, "You must be on your guard. You will be handed over to the local councils and flogged in the synagogues" (Mark 13:9). Church history tells us that every generation since the beginning of the church has suffered and many have died as martyrs. According to church tradition, most of the twelve disciples died for their faith. In the twentieth century alone, it is estimated that around twenty million people died because they were Christians. Persecution has been going on since the beginning of the church.

### 3. The Gospel Shared with the Nations

The third sign is "the gospel must first be preached to all nations" (Mark 13:10). The gospel is not just for one group. It is not just for the Jew, it is also for the Gentile; not just for the European, but also for the Asian; not just for the white, but also for people of all colors. During the last two thousand years, we have made much progress in spreading the gospel to the nations, but we are not finished. We desperately need frontier missionaries to complete the task.

As I read the New Testament, it seems obvious that the early believers felt they had fulfilled this sign of sharing the gospel with the Gentiles. I believe the most consistent understanding of Scripture is that Jesus could have returned at any time in the last two thousand years. He could come back at any moment, any day, any hour. Here are a few Scriptures that suggest this:

- "The end of all things is near. Therefore be clear minded and self-controlled so that you can pray" (1 Peter 4:7).
- "Dear children, this is the last hour" (1 John 2:18).
- "And do this, understanding the present time. The hour has come for you to wake up from your slumber, because our salvation is nearer now than when we first believed. The night is nearly over; the day is almost here. So let us put aside the deeds of darkness and put on the armor of light" (Rom. 13:11–12).

- "You too, be patient and stand firm, because the Lord's coming is near" (James 5:8).

Christians in the first century lived in the present hope that Christ could come at any moment.

## Why the Wait?

So the obvious question is: If Christ could come at any moment, why the delay? Why do we wait? Think about it; we spend most of our lives waiting. We wait for the right person to marry; we wait to have kids; we wait for the kids to grow up; we wait for retirement. I'm waiting for the Dallas Cowboys to win the Super Bowl again.

We wait for Jesus to come back—for this blessed hope to be fulfilled. Why all this waiting? Peter gives us some insight when he writes, "But do not forget this one thing, dear friends: With the Lord a day is like a thousand years, and a thousand years are like a day. The Lord is not slow in keeping his promise, as some understand slowness. *He is patient with you, not wanting anyone to perish, but everyone to come to repentance*" (2 Peter 3:8–9, italics mine).

God's perspective is different from ours. He wants everyone to experience life in him, and so he waits. There was an economist who read this passage and said to God: "Lord, is it true that a thousand years for us is just like one minute to you?" God said, "Yes." The economist said, "So a penny is like a million dollars to you, right?" God said, "Yes." And the economist said, "Well, Lord, will you give me one of those pennies?" "Yes," God said, "wait here a minute."

Patience is one of the most amazing character traits of God. He is called the "God of patience" (Rom. 15:5 KJV). The term *patience* (or *longsuffering*) is often translated as "slow to anger." This aspect of God is rarely mentioned because it is often lumped in with God's goodness and mercy. Though very similar, there are some distinctions. While God's mercy is seen through his favor to people who don't deserve it, God's patience is seen through his suspending judgment. Mercy is positively extended toward individuals; patience involves a disposition within oneself to hold back. God holds back the return of Jesus as an act of patience so that more people may come to love him.

This is another area in which God is so unlike me. Though you can't tell now, I was born with red hair. My sister overheard someone looking at me through the nursery window and saying, "Is that not the ugliest baby you have ever seen?" My sister let him have it, but it seems I was destined to have some issues! If you know anything about us redheads, we are often a little hot tempered and impatient. I hate waiting. I'll drive past restaurants if people are standing in line; I'll leave if the wait is more than a few minutes. My blood pressure rises if I wait very long in traffic. God is patient; I am not. I actually stopped praying for patience because I was afraid of what God would have to do to give it to me.

Yet God knows something deeply spiritual happens in us while we wait. The psalmist wrote, "I wait for the LORD, my soul waits, and in his word I put my hope. My soul waits for the LORD more than watchmen wait for the morning, more than watchmen wait for the morning" (Ps. 130:5–6). The night watchman doesn't do much. He is not digging ditches, selling items, achieving new goals, or building anything tangible. His role is about *being* as much as *doing*. He *is* the watchman. He scans the darkness for trouble or distress. He listens and observes. He trusts that dawn will come. He waits and hopes.

As Christians we wait and hope. We know that God's timetable is not ours, and we long for his return. Eugene Peterson reminds us: "Waiting does not mean doing nothing. It is not fatalistic resignation. It means going about our assigned tasks, confident that God will provide the meaning and the conclusions. It is not compelled to work away at keeping up appearances with a bogus spirituality. It is the opposite of desperate and panicky manipulations, of scurrying and worrying."[6] In our waiting we are transformed into Jesus' image. We wait because God is patient and he longs for people to be saved.

I have a hard time being content and grateful while I'm waiting. I do not naturally exude joy as I stand in line at the grocery store or the bank. Yet, as God's people, while we wait in this life for Christ's return, we are called to be content and grateful. Lewis Smedes calls it the "deep paradox" of hope.

To be content in whatever state we are in is the wisdom to accept with gratitude the experience of *not* having what we wish for. Mark this well. We *cannot* be content with the way things are as long as things are not the way we wish them to be. Or the way they ought to be. We can be content to live with our discontent until they get to be the way we hope they will be. Contented discontent is hope's *patient impatience.*[7]

At the same time, we are both discontent and content; we long for Christ's return and yet are at peace in our current circumstance. We strive to see him return, but we wait patiently in hope.

## Looking Forward with Anticipation

When I was fifteen, I heard someone speak about Christ's return being imminent. I remember thinking, *No, that can't happen. I have to get my driver's license first.* It was as though I thought he should work around my life plans to schedule his return. After I got my driver's license, I was pulled over one day. I thought I was in trouble for a lot more than a speeding ticket, and, as the police officer walked up to my car, I prayed, "Okay, Jesus, you can come now! Please! Please come now! Anytime in the next ten seconds would be great!" Obviously my relationship with God at that time was not very mature.

The New Testament has more than three hundred references to Christ's return. The overwhelming image the Bible uses is that of a wedding. John writes: "Let us rejoice and be glad and give him glory! For the wedding of the Lamb has come, and his bride has made herself ready. . . . Then the angel said to me, 'Write: "Blessed are those who are invited to the wedding supper of the Lamb!"' And he added, 'These are the true words of God'" (Rev. 19:7, 9). Notice the term *blessed* in the context of the wedding.

I remember my own wedding. After Lori agreed to marry me, our lives became a circus for the next four months. We had to plan a wedding, put together invitations, pick colors and songs, and, yes, disagree. I figured out early on that my best bet was to nod and smile. Everyone who has planned a wedding has at least flirted with the idea of eloping—even if it was only a one-second afterthought. I endured the planning, and found that on our wedding day it was worth it. When Lori walked down the aisle, she was absolutely beautiful. I smiled and thought about how I was getting the best end of the deal. As I took her hand, the joy was incomparable. All the preparations seemed minor at that moment. In much the same way, all of our struggles will be worth it on that glorious day when Christ returns.

This hope gives us the ability to laugh when our finan-
cial endeavors don't pan out and it frees us to cry without
despair. We can face each day with a sense of expectation
because we know that our experience here is not the final
verdict. Though God may seem distant now, someday we
will see him face-to-face. When we are disappointed, we
know someday we will understand. No matter how hard
life gets, we are bound for a better place. Jesus waits for
us, his bride, to meet him at the great wedding celebration
God has planned. And on the honeymoon there will be
no fighting, no fatigue, and, best of all, no end.

## Living in Outrageous Hope

A T-shirt reads: "Jesus is coming: Everybody look busy!"
He could come back before you finish reading it. Are you
ready? The reality is Jesus is coming, but how will he find
us living?

Christ's appearance will happen either during our life
or at the moment of our death. We should live each day
in light of this. As Augustine said, "He who loves the coming of the Lord is not he who affirms it is far off, nor is it
he who says it is near. It is he who, whether it be far or
near, awaits with sincere faith, steadfast hope, and fervent
love."[8]

Joseph Stowell recalls a time he visited a Christian home
for mentally handicapped children. When he walked in,
he saw that the window had handprints all over it. Stowell
commented to his friend: "Lots of handprints." His friend
replied, "The children here love Jesus, and they're so eager
for him to return that they lean against the windows as
they look up to the sky." When was the last time you
left handprints on the glass? When was the last time you

truly lived with hope and anticipation? Peter writes, "But in keeping with his promise we are looking forward to a new heaven and a new earth, the home of righteousness" (2 Peter 3:13).

"Yes," Lori said, and my life is so much richer for it. "Yes," God says, and our lives are transformed because of it.

## Questions for Discussion

1. Share a fun story about a wedding in which you were involved.
2. What emotion comes to your mind when you think of Jesus' return—fear or joy? Why?
3. A primary image God uses to teach us about Jesus' return and heaven is that of a wedding celebration. How should this influence how we view Jesus' return?
4. Read Mark 13:32–37. What does this tell us about predicting Jesus' return?
5. If God can return at any time for those who love him, we may wonder, *Why the delay?* Read 2 Peter 3:8–9. What insight does this passage give about the delay of Christ's return?
6. Why does the promise of Jesus' return give you hope?

# FOUR

# A HOPE THAT PURIFIES OUR LIVES

*Our best havings are our wantings.*[1]

C. S. LEWIS

Bryan felt out of place growing up. As a kid he wondered when the aliens would land in his front yard and announce, "Hi, Bryan, we're here to take you home." Externally things seemed fine. Growing up in a nice neighborhood, he had two pleasant parents and a great house. Yet on the inside, fear and emptiness disconnected him from reality.

At twelve, he loaded up on drugs for the first time. He suddenly felt connected to "reality." His anxiety eased. His fears faded. His emptiness numbed. He felt oddly "okay" and resolved to do whatever it took to maintain that feeling. By fifteen it took a lot. His daily regimen included alcohol balanced with assortments of LSD, PCP, heroin, cocaine, and crystal methamphetamines. He became the epitome of a teenage suburban junkie, scraping up money for drugs legally and illegally in any way he could.

He entered his first rehab at age seventeen. After two months officials felt he needed a longer stay at a rehab facility in Desert Hot Springs, California, so he went there. Even without drugs his addictive personality continued to develop. When he could not fill his life with drugs, he filled it with girls and cigarettes. After several violations, Bryan was dismissed from the rehab facility. His drug use continued until he hit bottom two years later.

The drugs that had seemed to liberate him now enslaved him. He said, "I reached the jumping-off point where I could no longer imagine life with or without the booze and drugs. I wanted to die. I don't mean suicide. I was so completely broken that I just wanted to sit down and die." For the first time he saw the reality of his addiction. In that moment Bryan prayed the simplest, most profound prayer of his life: "God, if you are there, help me."

The next day, June 12, he checked into a sober-living house. Over the next months he cleaned up his life, attended AA meetings, worked the Twelve Steps, and began to heal. Normalcy returned to his life. He learned to live sober.

Bryan matured, married, had children, and even began attending church. Describing himself as a "fringe Christian," he accepted who Jesus claimed to be but didn't put him at the center of his life or follow his teachings. Before long the hole in his life he'd spent years trying to fill was opening up again.

After eleven years of sobriety, Bryan felt ready to drink again. He began to lay a foundation for his relapse. He even planned to move across the country to get away from his AA friends.

But God had other plans. Through a series of circumstances, he discovered a Christ-centered recovery ministry. After he attended the first meeting, the pastor asked him to get involved leading a class. He thought, *What's going on here? I can't lead a Twelve-Step class. I've spent the last six months wanting to drink, all day, every day. Heck, I almost moved my entire family cross-country so I could feel less guilty about drinking again. And now I'm being asked to lead a Twelve-Step class?* Yet that moment of trust and responsibility became key in Bryan's ability to take strides toward God. He placed his hope in Jesus. He confessed to his wife and friends the plan he had devised to drink again. He surrendered his life to Christ and became part of a community that loved him unconditionally.

Bryan experienced the purifying power of hope. He set his hope on Jesus, not the next drink. He clung to the promise that one day he would be completely healed of the urge to drink. He grasped what John described: "Dear friends, now we are children of God, and what we will be has not yet been made known. But we know that when he appears, we shall be like him, for we shall see him as he is. Everyone who has this hope in him purifies himself, just as he is pure" (1 John 3:2–3).

Hope empowers obedience. The certain knowledge that God can and will fulfill his promises in the future inspires in us reverence and awe. As we realize grace waits to empower us in the future, we are motivated to love God more than we love sin. Hope set on heaven instills transforming power and clarity. We live toward the future and discover strength in the present. And even though fear of Jesus' returning and catching us in the act of sin has a purifying power, the primary hope John refers to is the hope of Jesus himself.

As that hope took root in Bryan's life, he experienced God in new and powerful ways. "I don't deserve this," he said. "What I deserve is to be six feet under. What I deserve is to be doing a stretch in one of our finer correctional facilities. What I deserve is to spend my days in a padded room because I never came down from the drugs. But what I received instead is the amazing grace and love of Jesus. I have a hope that will not let me down." Bryan is purified by his hope in Jesus.

Sin shall not have power over us in the age to come. We will be free as God is free, without sin. God alone will be our satisfaction. As Augustine notes, we will be "set free from delight in sinning to take unfailing delight in not sinning."[2] But until then, we struggle with sin.

**Loving God More than Sin**

A key motivating aspect to purity is realizing that happiness and joy are ultimately found only in God. He alone is the one who can satisfy our needs. John Piper writes:

> I find in the Bible a divine command to be a pleasure seeker—that is, to forsake the two-bit, low-yield, short-term, never-satisfying, person-destroying, God-belittling pleasures of the world and to sell everything "with joy" (Matt. 13:44) in order to have the kingdom of heaven,

and thus "enter into the joy of your master" (Matt. 25:21, 23). . . . The pursuit of pleasure is a necessary part of all worship and virtue.[3]

We do not bury the pursuit of pleasure when we become a Christian. Instead, we realize that pleasure is a gift from God and it is ultimately found in him—not simply in God's gifts but in him.

Solomon learned this lesson. Three thousand years ago he reigned over Israel for four decades of peace. He earned about twenty-five tons of gold a year, not including revenues from merchants, traders, Arabian kings, and governors of the land. We read that he "made silver as common in Jerusalem as stones, and cedar as plentiful as sycamore-fig trees in the foothills" (1 Kings 10:27).

In the book of Ecclesiastes Solomon writes what appear to be journal entries concerning his experiences of seeking pleasure and fulfillment in life apart from God. In those journals we see that he tried wisdom. He searched through the libraries and sought instruction from the teachers. When knowledge didn't satisfy, Solomon turned his attention to pleasure, and he had the finances to do it. He tried laughter, the party scene, comedy, sexual experiences, entertainment, building projects—you name it. His conclusion: "'Meaningless! Meaningless!' says the Teacher. 'Utterly meaningless! Everything is meaningless'" (Eccles. 1:2).

Solomon's term *meaningless* or *vanity* could also be translated "vapor" or "mist." The idea is that everything in life is without enduring substance. Like a mist that rises from the ground in the morning and disappears in the sun, so is all that Solomon experienced without God. In the end he says it all came down to mist, a puff of wind, a cold, empty nothing—vapor.

Pleasure is found in a purifying relationship with God. As Solomon concluded his journal: "Now all has been heard; here is the conclusion of the matter: Fear God and keep his commandments, for this is the whole duty of man" (Eccles. 12:13). He had searched and found that the happiness promised in all the material and sensual pleasures of life ultimately didn't satisfy. Solomon realized the importance of loving God more than sin. We need to ask questions similar to Solomon's. Do we love God more than sin? Do we really believe he can satisfy us completely? Do we find our joy in him more than in anyone else?

He alone can satisfy. Until we fully grasp this, purity will seem like a pleasure killer rather than the path to the greatest pleasure. Holiness may be hard, but its rewards are joy and true happiness.

**Pure in Heart**

Jesus linked purity with the future when he stated, "Blessed are the pure in heart, for they will see God" (Matt. 5:8). Many of the Beatitudes have both a now application and a future fulfillment, and purity is no exception. The pure in heart will one day behold the glory of God!

The word *heart* comes from the word *kardia,* from which we get *cardiac* and other words. The term refers to the seat of the motives and attitudes, the center of personality. It gets to the questions: What's really driving me? Whom am I trying to impress?

Happy are those whose motivations, whose whole heart, belong completely to God. As Dietrich Bonhoeffer said, "Who is pure in heart? Only those who have surrendered their hearts completely to Jesus that he may reign in them alone."[4] In this surrender there is great joy!

Purity is often defined negatively as the absence of impurity. We buy purified water, oil, and soaps that have had impurities filtered out of them. But biblical purity is both negative and positive. Its negative connotation is that it implies an absence of sinful attitudes and behaviors that destroy our lives. The pure in heart mourn over their sin, are bothered by their own unrighteousness, and long to be holy. James writes: "Come near to God and he will come near to you. Wash your hands, you sinners, and purify your hearts, you double-minded" (James 4:8). He challenges us to move toward God and, in doing so, drive out sin. The positive side of purity of heart is that it describes someone who finds delight in God, who focuses on God, and who loves holiness.

Søren Kierkegaard, the Danish philosopher, wrote the helpful book *Purity of Heart Is to Will One Thing*. For Kierkegaard purity of heart is essentially connected with one's focus—living each moment of life under the lordship of Jesus. When I first read the book in college, it drove me to my knees to seek God's power, to focus on his holiness, to strive to please him alone.

Appropriately Kierkegaard begins and ends the book with this prayer:

Father in heaven! What is a man without Thee! What is all that he knows, vast accumulation though it be, but a chipped fragment if he does not know Thee! What is all his striving, could it even encompass a world, but a half-finished work if he does not know Thee: Thee the One who are one thing and who are all! So may Thou give to the intellect, wisdom to comprehend that one thing; to the heart, sincerity to receive this understanding; to the will, purity that wills only one thing. In prosperity may Thou grant perseverance to will one thing; amid distractions, collectedness to will one thing; in suffering, patience to will one thing. Oh, Thou that giveth both the beginning and the completion, may Thou early, at the dawn of day, give to the young man the resolution to will one thing. As the day wanes, may Thou give to the old man a renewed remembrance of his first resolution, that the first may be like the last, the last like the first, in possession of a life that has willed only one thing.[5]

Purity of heart is a call to love God above all and to worship him with a focused, passionate heart; to remember him in prosperity, distractions, and suffering; to seek him at the dawn of day and as the day wanes. John emphasizes a similar thought when he writes, "And now, dear children, continue in him, so that when he appears we may be confident and unashamed before him at his coming" (1 John 2:28). The word *continue* means to abide or remain, in reference to a place. It also can have the idea of lodging somewhere over a period of time. By abiding in Jesus, we purify ourselves and prepare for his soon return. Notice John includes as part of our motivation of purity the hope of being unashamed at Jesus' return.

As we surrender to Jesus, we enter a close and abiding relationship with him. We continually think about him and pray to him. We are spiritually *in* him. We become so connected to him that we begin to grieve over what grieves him. We are convicted about what violates his goodness. Over and above all things, we desire him.

We take Jesus' teaching seriously. Jesus is the greatest intellect who ever lived, and we treasure his insight. No commentary takes his place. No teacher compares to him;

no guide is as sure. His brilliance becomes a part of our purifying process as he instills in us his wisdom.

Dallas Willard writes:

> "Jesus is Lord" can mean little in practice for anyone who has to hesitate before saying, "Jesus is smart." He is not just nice, he is brilliant. He is the smartest man who ever lived. He is now supervising the entire course of world history (Rev. 1:5) while simultaneously preparing the rest of the universe for our future role in it (John 14:2). He always has the best information on everything and certainly also on the things that matter most in human life.[6]

We do well to heed his words.

If you're like me, abiding in Christ is your desire but also your frustration. One day I am focused and passionate about seeking God from the moment I wake up. The next day I remember to pray as I climb into bed at night. The spirit is willing, but the flesh is weak. I long to enter into the consistency of following God each moment, but it eludes me. I want to set my ego and false motivations aside, but they creep back in. I want to love people freely with no strings attached, but my selfishness gets in the way. Purity of heart is as much a hope as a reality for most of us. We can be thankful that God looks at the heart. According to Jesus the good news is that this yearning for purity of heart comes with a promise: We will *see God.*

## Seeing His Glory

Purity in heart comes with an amazing reward, not only joy on earth but seeing God's face in the future. The thought of seeing God is astonishing. Moses longed to see God's face. He said to the Lord:

"Now show me your glory." And the LORD said, "I will cause all my goodness to pass in front of you, and I will proclaim my name, the LORD, in your presence. I will have mercy on whom I will have mercy, and I will have compassion on whom I will have compassion. But," he said, "you cannot see my face, for no one may see me and live."

Then the LORD said, "There is a place near me where you may stand on a rock. When my glory passes by, I will put you in a cleft in the rock and cover you with my hand until I have passed by. Then I will remove my hand and you will see my back; but my face must not be seen."

EXODUS 33:18–23

Even Moses, bold as he was, did not see God's face in his lifetime. Imagine looking at the face of the eternal Being—One who always has been and always will be, the Alpha and Omega, One whose wisdom and knowledge and glory are unfathomable! Jesus says the pure in heart will see God, experience God, and find their pleasure fully in God.

In the Old Testament, reference was made to the face to indicate both favor and disgrace. God's face was said to "shine" with favor (Ps. 4:6). And a lack of his favor was described as God's hiding his face. God turns his face toward the pure in heart; they see it and are satisfied. There is no higher honor than seeing God and delighting in him.

Every earthly pleasure is mixed with pain and disappointment. I love Mexican food, but when I indulge, I face the post-dinner heartburn. I love ice cream, but I feel guilty after devouring it. Every rose has its thorn. Every delight is mixed with frustration. Every pleasure comes to an end.

The pleasures of this life are fickle, but the pleasures of seeing God are not. He delivers his promise. As we perceive God's grace, we are humbled and grateful. As we perceive his power, we are moved and awed. As we perceive his patience, we are surprised and overjoyed. As we perceive his holiness, we are convicted and cleansed. As we perceive his goodness, we are softened and changed. Seeing his glory and love should bring our greatest happiness. No guilt will linger after this pleasure, no tortured conscience after this encounter. His glory pushes out sin, partially in this life but ultimately in the life to come. There we will experience complete satisfaction, and forever our pleasure increases as his glory reveals itself.

## Purity Flows from Grace

It is important to remember we do not purify ourselves to *earn* God's approval, but precisely the opposite. Because we have hope in his love and grace to meet our future need, we are purified. Out of the incredible resources we have as children of God, we are motivated to be pure. God already has made us right, clothed us with righteousness, transformed us. This is our present reality and future hope. To this grace we cling in the trenches of life.

In Romans 7 we have Paul's autobiography of his personal struggle for purity. He shares his feelings, his weaknesses, and his heart. He gives us a portrait of a struggling Christian and pulls the curtain back, allowing us to gaze into his soul. By looking at Paul's struggle, we learn valuable lessons about purity and hope.

"We know that the law is spiritual," Paul writes, "but I am unspiritual, sold as a slave to sin. I do not understand what I do. For what I want to do I do not do, but what I hate I do" (v. 14). To paraphrase, Paul says, "There is a civil war going on in my heart. I want to do what is good, but again and again I do not." Does that resonate with you? Most of us are plagued with personal contradictions. We want to do one thing but end up doing another. We want to be more disciplined but can't get started. We want to change but remain the same. We want to be more organized but remain in chaos.

The Bible says when we become a Christian we receive a new nature. The problem is that we still have our old nature to contend with, and that nature wants to sin. There is a war between these two natures. Sin, meaning actions that miss God's desire for our lives, wants to dominate us. In Romans 7 Paul uses the pronoun *I* twenty-seven times in twelve verses (vv. 14–25). He is trying to be right with God on his own, but, clearly, he can't be.

Have you ever asked yourself, *Why do I hurt the people I love the most? Why do I gossip when I resolve to hold my tongue? Why do I keep drinking when I say I will quit?* You're in good company. Paul says, "I do not understand what I do" (v. 15).

Here is Paul, one of the greatest Christian leaders of all time, a top-drawer mind, a person who was called up into the third heaven and saw things he could not speak of—but he does not understand what he does! He wants to do good, but nothing seems to change. The law is good, but he can't meet its requirements.

As Paul struggles with the law, he finally hits bottom. He writes, "What a wretched man I am! Who will rescue me from this body of death?" (v. 24). The term *wretched* literally means "worn out from exhaustion." He is at the end of his rope.

Paul's words remind me of one of the deepest, darkest moments of my life. I sought to do God's will and wanted to please him with a passion. Somehow, in the midst of all my zeal, I began the subtle move from a grace-based faith to a works-based faith. Almost subconsciously I began to think, *I can do this on my own. I can set some righteousness records. I can tip the balance of the scales of my life.* Inevitably I began to allow other people's rules to influence my life. I began to talk a certain way and act a certain way. Legalism killed my joy.

When Paul came to the end of his own righteousness, he asked the question: "Who will rescue me from this body of death?" In the ancient world, the phrase "body of death" carried with it some interesting history. Near Tarsus, Paul's birthplace, an ancient tribe dealt with murder very harshly. The convicted murderer was strapped to the dead body of the slain and remained joined to his victim until the decay of the corpse infected the murderer and killed him or her. Maybe this is what Paul refers to when he says, "body of death."[7] Paul is saying, "Who will rescue me from my sin nature that is strapped to me, from my habits that seem unbreakable, from my attitudes that baffle me?"

Then Paul almost explodes with his declaration of victory: "Thanks be to God—through Jesus Christ our Lord!" (v. 25). God alone can rescue us from ourselves and from the law. The Christian life is not hard; it's impossible! The only way you can live it is to let God's power live through you.

When I hit bottom, God subtly but powerfully reminded me, "It is not about you, Jud. It's about my Son. He fulfilled the requirement for righteousness. Put your faith in him and be clothed with that righteousness." When I began to do that, I experienced again the inner joy that had become clouded. Joy is about being free in grace. You can line up all your good works, but they ultimately will not earn your way with God. Put your faith and trust in the love of God. Only he can tip the balance of the scales of your life.

## Grace-Based Hope

In John Bunyan's classic work *The Pilgrim's Progress,* we read of Faithful, who is climbing up a hill called Difficulty. Suddenly a man coming toward him "as swift as an eagle" attacks him with a staff. The man strikes him with a terrible blow, and Faithful is knocked down. Getting up, Faithful asks why he was hit, and the man strikes him again so forcefully it knocks him unconscious. When he comes to, he cries for mercy, but the man says, "The law knows no mercy." With that he prepares to strike him with the deathblow. Then a man walks by and tells the man with the staff to desist. Faithful says at first he does not know the man who saved him, "but as He went by I saw scars in His hands and feet, and I knew He was our Lord." As for the man with the staff, he was Moses, for the law will break you.[8]

The law is a good thing; we just can't keep it. When we move from living a grace-based life to a works-based life, we are setting up all kinds of external laws and hoops that we believe will earn favor with God. But the real answer to finding favor with God is found in Romans 8, which talks about God's Spirit working in us. It begins with wonderful words: "Therefore, there is now no condemnation for those who are in Christ Jesus" (v. 1).

Dietrich Bonhoeffer writes:

> Happy are they who have reached the end of the road we seek to tread, who are astonished to discover the by no means self-evident truth that grace is costly just because it is the grace of God in Jesus Christ. Happy are the simple followers of Jesus Christ who have been overcome by his grace, and are able to sing the praises of the all-sufficient grace of Christ with humbleness of heart. . . . Happy are

they who know that discipleship simply means the life which springs from grace, and that grace simply means discipleship. Happy are they who have become Christians in this sense of the word. For them the word of grace has proved a fount of mercy.[9]

God's grace in our lives is received freely, but that does not mean it costs nothing. In fact his grace cost Jesus everything and in a real sense it costs us everything. We do not earn grace; we respond to it, but we respond to it with our whole lives. Grace should motivate us to discipleship, not apathy, in our spiritual lives. Because of grace we are empowered to be pure and to love God more than we love sin.

## Questions for Discussion

1. What are some things our culture engages in to discover happiness?
2. How should our belief that happiness and joy come when we love God change our behavior?
3. When you think of the word *pure,* what comes to mind?
4. Jesus said, "Blessed are the pure in heart, for they will see God" (Matt. 5:8). What does Jesus mean?
5. What does it mean to say purity flows from grace?
6. How can hope inspire us to live pure lives?

# FIVE

# A HOPE THAT RELEASES BITTERNESS

*Christ spoke of faith, hope, love, and forgiveness. And these are things I think we need to be reminded of again. He forgave as he was tortured and killed. And we could do with a little of that behavior.*[1]

MEL GIBSON

Why didn't you help me that night?" asked Nancy. The words pierced Mike's heart. Filled with anguish and pain, they hung in the air. He was speechless.

Nancy, now a mature adult, recounted a terrifying childhood at the hands of their father. For years she and her sisters were sexually molested; all the children were abused.

Nightly their father would put a chair in the middle of the kitchen floor and line up the children. Their mom gave the daily report of wrongs: "Mike spilled his milk"; "Nancy left her sweater on the bedroom floor." Their father proceeded to beat them mercilessly. Each night it was the same, and the children assumed this was normal behavior.

In a counseling session Mike recalled an incident. One Sunday morning Mike's father mentioned that Mike had sleepwalked the night before. Mike could not remember. But sitting in that counseling room, hearing Nancy, the memory returned. He had walked into the room, looked at Nancy, and walked out. Then subconsciously he blocked out what he had seen—his father molesting his younger sister on the floor.

Mike and Nancy were born and raised in a suburb of Chicago in a family of six children. Their parents were devout Catholics. Their father demanded they pray the rosary every night and go to confession every Saturday and church every Sunday. Yet life was filled with conflict and contradictions. The family looked caring and loving, but their souls were empty. They needed God, but they feared him too much to embrace him. The children had one image of a father, and that image terrified them. So Mike, Nancy, and their other siblings did not get involved with Catholicism beyond what was demanded. They kept their distance from the priest and lived in fear of both their father and religion.

His father's abuse caused Mike to develop a sense of inadequacy and mixed feelings toward his father. He hated the things his father did but still cared for his parent. As an adult, he desired his father's approval and love more than anything but avoided developing a close relationship with him.

Mike graduated from high school and married within two years. Earning degrees in business and marketing, he landed what appeared to be a great job in New York City. But the move complicated his life and marriage.

Finally Mike faced the bitterness he felt toward his father. He said, "I determined that my holding on to any kind of bitterness or unforgiveness was tearing me to shreds. If I was going to be anything in my life, anything for my family, I needed to let go of the bitter and get better. If I stayed in that spot, it would kill me and I'd end up being useless to everyone."

With a coworker Mike attended a Billy Graham crusade. He learned that God loves him, sent his Son to die for him, and wants a relationship with him. As Graham invited people to come forward, Mike remained glued to his seat. He wanted to accept Christ, but something held him back. Over the next couple of weeks he asked his coworker many questions: What about hate and evil in the world? Where is God when the innocent suffer? Where was God when my sisters suffered? What does it mean to say God is a loving father?

On his natural birthday, June 15, Mike accepted Christ into his life. He felt thrilled at his new faith and hope. But his spiritual joy was soon dampened by a startling revelation—his wife was having an affair. The pain of neglect from his childhood returned, threatening to overwhelm him. After a year of counseling, his wife informed him they had grown apart and had different goals. Eventually they divorced, and Mike struggled through one of the most difficult periods of his life. "I knew that God would never leave me," he said. "God loves my children more than I do. He would work for our good because I was trusting him and living according to his purposes."

Nine years after his conversion, Mike was laid off from his job. After searching extensively for a new job, he decided to move back to Chicago. While there he tried to improve the relationship he had with his parents. He had worked through a process of forgiveness, but he didn't realize how bad the abuse had been or the damage it had done until he sat in the counseling session with his sister: "Why didn't you help me that night?" All the pent-up pain and anguish resurfaced in a moment—the sense of fear he had lived with, the beatings he had endured, the things he had seen. All he could say to his sister was, "I don't know." When he had seen his sister being abused, he walked away. But now he would not walk. This time he would help her. This time he would confront his father. Anger toward his father and personal disappointment boiled within him. He had to make things right.

After leaving the counselor's office, Mike drove to his parents' home and demanded they get in the car and drive to a session with his brothers and sisters that very day. As amazing as it may seem, Mike's father agreed. The siblings and the parents met with the counselor. Mike's dad broke down in the session. He told them about his own abuse as a child, relaying one horror story after another. Finally, his father spoke words they desperately needed to hear: "I did it. I am so sorry." And he wept. Mike's mother sat stunned, almost in denial. She knew nothing of the sexual abuse.

Mike says, "I can't tell you how important it was for my sisters to hear my father's words." Over time, each of the children came to a place of forgiveness toward their parents. And Mike's mom was able to forgive his dad. They could not ignore what he had done or act as if nothing had happened—yet by God's grace the siblings were able to move forward and salvage the health of their own families and find healing together.

Following that session, Mike met weekly for lunch with his parents. He saw their hearts soften toward Jesus. Many times he wondered if the purpose of his move to Chicago was to lead his parents to faith.

One summer day Mike's seventy-eight-year-old father asked if he would help him come to know Jesus. Mike experienced the overwhelming privilege of leading his father to faith in Christ. Within a few moments of leaving his parents' home, Mike called his brothers and sisters, who were Christ-followers, and informed them of what had happened. Initially they were skeptical, but over time they watched their father's transformation into a loving, gentle, committed believer in Jesus. He had been illiterate all his life, but now he wanted to learn to read so he could study God's Word for himself—and he did!

One year later, sitting around a restaurant table at lunch, Mike and his father passionately shared their faith with Mike's mom. Mike sat in awe as his "rough and tough" dad relayed the message of forgiveness and grace that could be hers. At seventy-four, she felt ready. Mike's dad kept telling her of her need for Christ until she said, "Would you shut up so I can pray?" There, in the restaurant, as her hands trembled, she repeated a prayer to accept Christ into her life and to start again.

Mike and his family discovered the hope that releases bitterness. As the members of his family surrendered to Jesus, each was transformed by hope. They were all freed from the bitterness that threatened to destroy their lives.

## The Price of Bitterness

Bitterness and unforgiveness have tremendous psychological and physical ramifications in our lives. One article in the *New York Times* reported: "Researchers have gathered a wealth of data lately, suggesting that chronic anger is so damaging to the body that it ranks with or even exceeds cigarette smoking, obesity, and a high fat diet as a powerful risk factor for early death."[2]

Another study at the University of North Carolina tracked twenty-five men for a period of years and concluded that hidden hostility made them six times more likely to die than those who had forgiven others.[3] The longer we allow our anger to build up, the more devastating are its effects. Frederick Buechner writes:

> Of the Seven Deadly Sins, anger is possibly the most fun. To lick your wounds, to smack your lips over grievances long past, to roll over your tongue the prospect of bitter confrontations still to come, to savor to the last toothsome morsel both the pain you are given and the pain you are giving back—in many ways it is a feast fit for a king. The chief drawback is that what you are wolfing down is yourself. The skeleton at the feast is you.[4]

If we let our anger brew, we are only hurting ourselves. When anger and bitterness get a foothold in our lives, we miss much of the joy we could experience.

As I reflect on my own experience with bitterness and anger, I find that the only people my anger truly hurts are my loved ones and me. Anger causes me to adopt a "you owe me" attitude toward others. It starts with the person I am angry with, but soon it takes on a life of its own and is projected onto the world. The longer I allow it to develop, the more I become mad at the world. I move beyond moments of anger and become an angry person, and my attitude colors everything and every relationship. In a short time this brooding can explode and cause all kinds of damage.

I have counseled people so caught up in anger that they can't see their own responsibility for their dilemma. They blame everything in their lives on someone or something else—parents, children, spouse, relatives, their job. They are consumed with anger and refuse to deal with the truth. Until they make an effort to come to a place of forgiveness toward others, they will never be happy—never.

I understand how difficult forgiveness can be. It does not happen instantly but is a process, especially if the hurt runs deep. Forgiveness may even seem impossible, but the sooner we begin the journey toward forgiveness, the sooner we will be free.

We have to lay our anger down before God. He will settle the score in his own way. He has forgiven us so much that we have no alternative but to offer forgiveness to those who have wronged us. When we let go of anger, the freedom and power we feel is indescribable. It opens us up to experience life at its best.

**Future Justice**

Some conclude that forgiveness ignores justice. Shouldn't Mike's dad pay for what he did? Yet forgiveness neither ignores justice nor implies that a person shouldn't face consequences. In fact God commands us to forgive because he has dealt with the justice issue directly. Jesus died so that God could "demonstrate his justice at the present time, so as to be just and the one who justifies those who have faith in Jesus" (Rom. 3:26). Jesus' death allows God to forgive me and still punish sin. Jesus bore the consequences of justice. Christ has already paid for the sin of believers who wrong me, and one day God will settle accounts with unbelievers. Jesus understood that all sin would be paid for, either on the cross or in eternity.

Often the Bible speaks of Jesus' coming in terms of his being a judge. He is "the one whom God appointed as judge of the living and the dead" (Acts 10:42). We usually think of a judge in a negative or fearful way. Over the years I have worked my share of summer church camps. At one camp, I was amazed at how well the kids were responding to my authority. I told them to do something, and they did it. When I told them it was time for bed, they went to bed. If I told them to take showers, they took showers. Just as I was starting to get used to this radical behavior, one of the kids came up to me and said, "Sir, since you are the judge, what happens if we get in trouble?"

"What do you mean?" I asked.

"Well, everybody calls you 'judge,'" he said. "I was wondering what you do to us if we mess up."

Suddenly it all clicked: the kids had heard my name as "Judge" instead of "Jud." That was why they were jumping at my every word. Trying to keep my composure, I replied to this little boy, "Just do what you're supposed to, have a good time, and don't worry about it." Hey, this judge thing was working so well I thought I would milk it for all it was worth!

In ancient times the term *judge* referred to more than a member of the judicial system, and it did more than inspire fear. The term carried with it the idea of leadership. When the Judge of the living and the dead comes, justice will come for the poor, the alien, the downtrodden, and those who cannot defend themselves. All the ledgers will be balanced. The accounts will be paid. Justice will be served. Wrongs will be made right.

John writes in Revelation about the overthrow of Babylon, the city that represents the world network of religions, economies, and governments that is against God. As God's judgment is poured out on Babylon, John writes, "Rejoice over her, O heaven! Rejoice, saints and apostles and prophets! God has judged her for the way she treated you" (Rev. 18:20). A few verses later all of heaven shouts, "Hallelujah! Salvation and glory and power belong to our God, for true and just are his judgments" (Rev. 19:1–2). We rejoice not in seeing others suffer, but in the finality of the struggle. We rejoice because evil is banished from the world and a new day dawns. We rejoice because justice finally is administered for the sake of believers. We rejoice because the world is judged "for the way she treated you." For Christians brutalized and killed, for the believer unjustly destroyed, for the one denied justice at every turn—a day of reckoning will come.

Paul says, "Therefore judge nothing before the appointed time; wait till the Lord comes. He will bring to light what is hidden in darkness and will expose the motives of men's hearts. At that time each will receive his praise from God" (1 Cor. 4:5). Justice will break forth in the best sense, which is something we look forward to. Those who wronged you will be discovered. Being assured of God's justice means our anger can give way to forgiveness, and despair can give way to hope. God will do what is right.

## Hope and Forgiveness

Forgiveness cuts against our natural inclinations. Once, in preparation for a talk on forgiveness, I purchased a

95

book—*The Revenge Encyclopedia*—that offers almost one thousand ways to get even. The book is full of ideas, even ideas on how to get back at your minister. While these examples are extreme, most of us find much more subtle ways to get even. We don't need *The Revenge Encyclopedia* because we keep score well enough on our own.

Maybe we struggle with our children—words they've spoken, life choices they've made, clothes they wear. Overnight they went from being sweet, loving children to aliens. Perhaps we haven't forgiven our spouse. He always leaves his socks on the floor; she never puts the lid on the toothpaste. He never talks with me; she isn't interested in me physically. He has zero romance; she doesn't support my work. Soon these things add up, and bitterness gets a foothold in our lives.

We also can be bitter toward God. When our dreams don't materialize, when roadblocks continue to get in the way, our hearts can grow hard and bitter toward the very One we serve.

Unforgiving attitudes will squelch relationships in our marriage, home, workplace, and church. Lorne Sanny, for many years president of the Navigators, says that bitterness has put more people on the shelf in their service to God than any other thing he knows. He describes bitterness as "a sort of self-cannibalism" that eats your insides out.[5]

In the strongest language, Jesus links our own forgiveness with the way we forgive others: "For if you forgive men when they sin against you, your heavenly Father will also forgive you. But if you do not forgive men their sins, your Father will not forgive your sins" (Matt. 6:14–15).

We do not earn our forgiveness by forgiving others, but the surest sign that we have been forgiven is the way we forgive others. So unforgiveness is a huge issue in our lives. Until we get a grip on it, our relationships will not deepen, our hearts will not expand, our churches will not become all God desires for them. One of Satan's strategies is to exploit the lack of forgiveness among God's people: "I have forgiven in the sight of Christ for your sake," Paul writes, "in order that Satan might not outwit us. For we are not unaware of his schemes" (2 Cor. 2:10–11).

The problem all of us face is that forgiveness is not natural. Tell the mom whose son was killed by a drunken driver to forgive, or the husband whose wife faces a terminal illness and who struggles with bitterness toward God. Tell the woman to forgive who gives birth in a hospital room alone because her husband walked out on her, or the person who can't buy Christmas gifts for his children because he was laid off. Speak of forgiveness to the pastor after his leaders agreed that they should change the music style to reach younger families but then cave in to a few people who are upset by the change. Consider war or a tragedy such as 9/11—is forgiveness possible? C. S. Lewis said, "Every one says forgiveness is a lovely idea, until they have something to forgive, as we did during the war."[6] The process of coming to forgiveness can be excruciatingly difficult and painful, but the price of unforgiveness is greater.

## Check Out Your Credit History

In Matthew 18:21 Peter comes to Jesus with a personal question about the limits of forgiveness. He asks, "How many times shall I forgive my brother when he sins against me? Up to seven times?" Peter thinks he is being very gracious. To forgive seven times was more than twice what the rabbis taught. Jesus answered: "I tell you, not seven times, but seventy-seven times" (v. 22). Jesus was speaking of repeated, regular acts of wrongdoing toward someone many times a day, day after day. In each case a Christian's response is to forgive. Our forgiveness must never be surpassed by someone's wrongdoing. Then he breaks it down by telling us a story about a servant who owed a king ten thousand talents. This was equivalent to millions of dollars, an amount that could never be repaid. The servant and his family are ordered locked up until the debt is satisfied. "The servant fell on his knees before him. 'Be patient with me,' he begged, 'and I will pay back everything.' The servant's master took pity on him, canceled the debt and let him go" (v. 26). Suddenly this servant went from facing bondage and slavery to experiencing freedom and grace. He went from a future of hopelessness to hope, from darkness to light.

In Jesus' story the king is God and we are the debtors. God has forgiven us an amazing debt that we could never have repaid. Every evil thought, act, motive, and word has been forgiven. Each exaggerated truth, off-color joke, and cynical rant has been forgotten. When I lose compassion for others who have wronged me, I simply remember my own credit history with God, which reveals plenty of sin but also the amazing blessing of God's forgiveness.

My wife and I rarely argue, but we've had our spats. Once I had an argument with her that was clearly my fault. To this day she can't remember what the argument was about; all she remembers is that I walked out of the room.

As we argued, my frustration rose, so I left the room and went downstairs. I knew it would hurt her. And as I sat there sulking, with a terrible attitude toward the most important person in my life, my two-year-old daughter ran up to me and hugged me and said, "I love you, Daddy." There I was filled with sin, ugliness, and bitterness, and God sent such an amazing blessing to me. God could have struck me dead and been justified, but instead he blessed me. When I remember God's amazing gift to me, I am softened and open to change. That day I went upstairs and ate crow. And I'm glad I did.

## Resign as the Repo Man

Emilio Estevez starred in the 1984 movie *Repo Man.* His character roamed the streets collecting on people's bad debts. In Jesus' story in Matthew 18, we meet another "repo man." The servant who has just been forgiven a multimillion-dollar debt goes out to a person who owes him an infinitesimally small amount in comparison and demands repayment. According to the text, he began to choke his debtor. The man begged for mercy but was refused and was thrown into prison until he could pay what he owed.

Other servants who saw this were so disturbed that they told the king. Jesus said, "Then the master called the servant in. 'You wicked servant,' he said, 'I canceled all that debt of yours because you begged me to. Shouldn't you have had mercy on your fellow servant just as I had on you?'" (Matt. 18:32–33).

There is a repo person in every man and woman, a part of us that wants to even the score and collect our due. Sometimes it is not enough for us to just get even; we want to see someone truly suffer.

Yet I believe a question we will face on judgment day is this: "Shouldn't you have had mercy on your fellow servant just as I (God) had on you?"

Peter says we are to follow Jesus' example. "When they hurled their insults at him, he did not retaliate; when he suffered, he made no threats. Instead, he entrusted him-

99

self to him who judges justly" (1 Peter 2:23). In complete faith Jesus gave himself to God. In essence he said, "God, you know." When we are wronged, we entrust ourselves to the one who judges justly. When we take hits, we say, "God, you know!" When we are threatened, "God, you know!" When we are frustrated, "God, you know!" When we are criticized, "God, you know!"

Paul writes, "Do not take revenge, my friends, but leave room for God's wrath, for it is written: 'It is mine to avenge; I will repay,' says the Lord" (Rom. 12:19). Paul is saying God is the judge and he will settle accounts. We don't have to have the last word; we don't have to get even; we don't have to keep score. We don't have to win or try to salvage our reputation through retaliating. We are about God's fame and making his name great. We are about declaring his renown, and that happens when people see how radical our love and forgiveness are. We must entrust ourselves to the one who judges justly.

In Jesus' story in Matthew 18, the king finds out what the man who was forgiven so much did. Not only does the king confront the man, the Bible says, "In anger his master turned him over to the jailers to be tortured, until he should pay back all he owed. This is how my heavenly Father will treat each of you unless you forgive your brother from your heart" (vv. 34–35).

The repo man found himself shackled to a prison wall, totally bankrupt. He would rot there until he paid back all he owed.

## Forgiveness and Responsibility

We often struggle with forgiveness because we feel that the offender might not deserve forgiveness. Some think forgiveness implies reunion. But we don't have to let the person who wronged us back into our close circle of friends, and we're not called to restore a relationship that totally ignores the harm a person has done. Forgiveness does not even imply trust. Trust must be earned over a period of time. Forgiveness means I surrender my personal right to retaliate and trust God to fulfill justice. We forgive because unforgiveness hurts us more than it hurts anyone else.

**The Power of Forgiveness**

Bryan and Rachel Curtis discovered the power of forgiveness after much struggle. Rachel had become so frustrated with her husband that she ended up pointing a borrowed .38-caliber pistol at his sleeping body. *Bang!* The first shot grazed Bryan's neck. He sat up, looked at his wife and frantically tried to get out of bed. The second shot went through his shoulder. The next through his wrist. Two more shots hit him in the chest. Rachel was tired of his marijuana and his lies. She had already packed her bags and put their eighteen-month-old baby in the car. Click. Click. She was out of bullets.

He rushed her and grabbed the gun. Almost immediately, Rachel came to her senses and began to apologize. Bryan lay down; she called 911. As Bryan was rushed to the hospital, Rachel was rushed to jail.

With surgery, Bryan pulled through; Rachel was let out on bond. According to the way the world turns, this is where the lawsuits should begin and the divorce lawyers should be hired. The newspaper headlines should expose the layers upon layers of bitterness and revenge. But not for Bryan and Rachel. After being released from the

101

hospital, Bryan called Rachel, and an amazing process of forgiveness and healing began. The road was rough over the next several months. Thanks to God's intervention, they met my next-door neighbor, Dale Travis. Dale, a minister in our city, helped Bryan and Rachel find new life in Christ. Over time they both were able to forgive the other. Bryan refused to testify against Rachel, and attempted murder charges were dropped. He says, "I just figured if God could forgive me for the life I was living and give me a second chance at life, then I could give her a second chance."[7]

If Bryan and Rachel discovered how to forgive in such extreme circumstances, could we not discover it in our own situations?

**The Release of Bitterness**

Coming to the place of forgiveness, and the release from bitterness that results, does not happen overnight. We must spend time in prayer, asking for God's help, and then we must wait on God to work.

*Pray*

Jesus taught his disciples to pray, "Forgive us our debts, as we also have forgiven our debtors" (Matt. 6:12). Augustine labeled this request "the terrible petition" because if we pray, "Forgive us our sins, for we also forgive everyone who is indebted to us" but at the same time harbor an unforgiving spirit, we are actually asking God not to forgive us.

Prayer has a tremendous way of softening me. It allows me to see my part and to own my share of the responsibility for what has happened. I find that prayer cuts through my smoke screen and reveals my true heart. Corrie ten Boom wrote: "I discovered that it is not on our forgiveness any more than on our goodness that the world's healing hinges, but on His. When He tells us to love our enemies, He gives, along with the command, the love itself."[8]

### God Will Work

Forgiveness is a process; it takes time. Sometimes people forgive too quickly, without first really grieving and working through the process with God. In a mall we see a child hit another. As the tears flow, the mom jumps into the middle of the fray. "Say you're sorry," she says to the culprit. "Say it . . . one . . . two. . . ." "I'm sorry," the little guy says at 2.9 seconds. Mom turns to the other sibling, "Now, you say, 'I forgive you.'" With folded arms and clenched teeth he says, "I forgive you."

Children go through the steps of forgiveness but often hold the grudge in their hearts—at least until they forget about it. As adults we can go through the steps but we don't forget about it, nor are we asked to forget the offense. Our responsibility is to forgive, not forget. Until we go through the steps *and* forgive from the heart (Matt. 18:35), we won't find healing. If you've been angry for years, get some help. Don't be afraid of Christian counseling. Work through those issues, because there is tremendous freedom on the other side.

For twenty-two years Mike Warnke was the world's number one Christian comedian. He performed around the globe to sellout crowds. His books and tapes were consistent best-sellers. He had money to do anything he desired and a private plane to fly anywhere he wished to go. His ministry staff numbered more than fifty employees. Then in 1992 a Christian magazine looked behind the scenes of Warnke's life. They questioned his testimony, especially his claims to have been involved in Satanism before his conversion, and they uncovered abuses in his ministry. The fallout was quick and devastating. His performance schedule evaporated. Book and tape labels discontinued his products. The secular and Christian press ferociously attacked him. Within a few months he had lost all of his wealth and become an emotional basket case. He would stand in line at a grocery store with coupons for toilet paper and baked beans but not enough money for both.

Warnke has admitted his life was totally out of order. He had made decisions based on the bottom line rather than spiritual priorities. He admitted to exaggeration of his testimony and to the ungodliness of his personal life, to multiple divorces, and to unwise decisions. He got help from a group of spiritual advisers who independently investigated his life and ministry. At the time we spoke, he had been submitting to the accountability of this group for ten years. He wrote: "There were times I felt so alone. The hurt was so deep, the pain so palpable. To most of the Christian community I was *persona non grata*. . . . It was early in those dark days when I stood on my deck . . . and cried to God, 'You know!'"[9]

At one point he attended the annual convention of the Christian Booksellers Association. A believer walked up to him with rage in his eyes. He got in Warnke's face and let him have it: "How could you dare to show your face around here after what you did? You're an absolute disgrace to the body of Christ. You're not worthy to breathe the same air as the rest of the Christians here."

Warnke maintained his composure, looked the man in the eye, and said, "Sir, you are absolutely right. You've rebuked me; now restore me."[10] The guy stood there speechless for a few moments, then turned and walked away. Whom do you need to restore, to forgive? About whom are you harboring bitter thoughts? Who has wronged you? Make an effort to bring closure to each situation. Talk with the person and forgive him or her in your heart.

Forgiving someone because God forgave you: priceless. There are some things money can't buy.

**Questions for Discussion**

1. When you hear the term *judge,* what comes to your mind?
2. The Bible says Jesus is the judge of the living and the dead. Why should this inspire in us more hope than fear?
3. Who is hurt by our bitterness—the one we are bitter toward or ourselves?
4. Does forgiveness ignore justice? Does forgiveness imply that there must be reunion with the offender?
5. How can trusting in the future justice of God help us forgive now?
6. What are some steps you can take when you don't know how to forgive?
7. Share a time when you forgave someone. Was it difficult? How did you feel after forgiving the person?

# SIX

# A Hope That Transforms Suffering

*One so often hears people say, "I just can't handle it," when they reject a biblical image of God. . . . If we seek a God we can "handle," that will be exactly what we get. A God we can manipulate, suspiciously like ourselves, the wideness of whose mercy we've cut down to size.*[1]

KATHLEEN NORRIS

Several years ago I asked the staff of a church I served, "Whom do you admire most next to Jesus?" I received all kinds of answers: Billy Graham, Mother Teresa, Mom, Dad, spouse. Other than Billy Graham, the only name that appeared several times was one I had not expected:

Jim. I could not have agreed more, but it still caught me off guard to see his name among the others on this list of world changers.

Jim is in some ways still a long-haired hippie at heart—without the hair. He teaches a Bible class that has grown to include more than one hundred adults, and he serves as an elder in overseeing the spiritual dimension of his church. He is a servant who loves people. Jim is a light to the world, but people's greatest admiration for him is not because of any of these things.[2]

Jim loves his wife, Lana. They married in 1977. After a couple years of marriage, Lana began to have some trouble. She would experience slight paralysis or uncontrollable shaking, but the doctors could not make a diagnosis. In 1981 she was officially diagnosed with multiple sclerosis.

Lana taught mentally disabled kids in second and third grade. She loved them dearly, but her shaking continued to progress until she had to quit. Jim and Lana prayed, "God heal us; take the MS away."

One night they received a phone call from some friends who told them that God did not want Lana to be sick. If they would simply pray in faith, she would be healed. Jim says, "It sounded like there were two options: healed or sick. There was no in-between. That triggered something in me, and I saw how God was working through us in spite of everything."

He recalled how people would come up to Lana everywhere and tell her what an inspiration she was to them. They would tell her that, as they saw her coping with her condition, they realized they could handle their problems as well. God was using Jim and Lana in their suffering. "That night in 1987," Jim says, "our prayers changed from 'God heal us,' to 'God use us and help us cope.'"

Throughout her physical deterioration, Lana took life in stride. She was never mad at God. Though she wanted to be healed, she was thankful God could use her in her illness. People came to her constantly saying, "We love to see your smile. You give us so much courage!" Of course the frustration of disability took its toll. One night in the late 1980s, Lana broke down. Jim came home and found Lana lying on the couch in tears.

"What's the matter?" he asked.

"I have always given blood at the blood drive," she replied, "but today I was turned away. They don't even want my blood anymore." The fact that she could not contribute broke her heart. But even though Lana could not contribute as she once could, God only multiplied her influence as hope to the world. She clung to the God of hope in the middle of heartbreaking conditions.

As the years wore on, Jim reached a point where he was waking up five or six times a night to help Lana to the bathroom or to get medication for her when she could not sleep. The fatigue was building, and the strain was real. Finally, he placed Lana in an assisted-living facility. It was one of the toughest decisions of his life. He visits her consistently and seeks to ensure that she receives good care, but he admits he would not have been able to handle it if it were not for God and other Christians. Jim and Lana learned where to turn when fears become reality. They have placed their hope in God and clung to him as a refuge.

## Blessing through Suffering

All of us face suffering in life, some more than others. One of the most amazing word pictures that God gives us is in Psalm 56:8. David writes: "You have seen me tossing and turning through the night. You have collected all my tears and preserved them in your bottle! You have recorded every one in your book" (TLB). God is so moved by the sorrows of his children that the Bible presents the image of God collecting and putting our tears in a bottle. He records them in his book. Our pain is not wasted. It is not forgotten or meaningless.

Sometimes we suffer due to illness or tragedy, but Jesus also connected suffering with persecution. He said, "Blessed are those who are persecuted because of righteousness, for theirs is the kingdom of heaven. Blessed are you when people insult you, persecute you and falsely say all kinds of evil against you because of me. Rejoice and be glad, because great is your reward in heaven, for in the same way they persecuted the prophets who were before you" (Matt. 5:10–12).

This is the last of Jesus' famous Beatitudes, where he outlines the blessed life. *Blessed* means "fortunate, lucky, or happy." Its meaning is deeper than our modern usage of *happy*, for it points to something more comprehensive, involving the divine favor of God and the spiritual joy he imparts.

As I type the word *blessed* into my word processor's thesaurus, I am shocked by the number of synonyms that come up: *anoint, bestow, blissful, celestial, charmed, consecrate, divine, favor, grace, hallow, happy, holy, prosperous, revere, smile, serendipitous, venerate, worship*. It just goes to show how broad the term can be.

In extrabiblical literature, the Greek term translated "blessed" referred to those who were socially wealthy—the people who supposedly lived above the normal struggles others faced. The term was also used to describe the Greek gods. They were thought to exist in a state of bliss and contentment because they could have whatever they wanted. The English word *blessed* assimilated over time with the word *bliss* and came to refer to spiritual joy or happiness. Though *blessed* means more than happy, it certainly does not mean less.

In essence Jesus is saying, "Happy are the persecuted." What a reversal of our usual assumptions! Twice Jesus calls the persecuted "blessed" in this Beatitude. It is as if he is saying, "Double blessing to those who are persecuted." This state of blessedness produces joy, but not because of the pain we experience. Our joy comes because we know that the reward for suffering is great in the kingdom of heaven. This hope becomes the motivating factor for rejoicing. Jesus tells us that when we suffer for him we should "be glad" (Matt. 5:12). The term means "to exult, to rejoice greatly, and to be overjoyed." "Be glad" literally means to skip and jump with excitement, to leap for joy!

In Acts we read of Paul and Silas in prison. "About midnight Paul and Silas were praying and singing hymns to God, and the other prisoners were listening to them" (Acts 16:25). Even under house arrest, Paul openly praised God. He writes: "Rejoice in the Lord!" (Phil. 3:1). Hope transformed a terrible situation into something filled with God's joy and peace.

When Jesus called the persecuted blessed, he wasn't being glib about persecution. Within the next forty years, the persecutions of Nero would break out and Christianity would undergo one of the most intense times of persecution in its history. According to John Foxe, "Nero nicely refined upon cruelty, and contrived all manner of punishments for his victims. He had some sewed up in the skins of wild beasts, and then devoured by dogs till they expired; and others dressed in shirts made stiff with wax, fixed to axle-trees, and set on fire in his garden. This persecution was general throughout the Roman Empire; but it increased rather than diminished the spirit of Christianity."[3] Jesus knew that a day would come when people on that hillside, especially the Twelve, would pay dearly for their faith, and he wanted them to know they would be rewarded.

Persecution of Christians continues today. An estimated two hundred million Christians around the world are persecuted yearly because of what they believe. Michael Horowitz, the widely known and influential Jew, writes:

> The mounting persecution of Christians eerily parallels the persecution of Jews, my people, during much of Europe's history. . . . The silence and indifference of Western elites to the beatings, looting, torture, jailing, enslavement, murder, and even crucifixion of increasingly vulnerable Christian communities further engages my every bone and instinct as a Jew. My grandparents and those who lived with them in the ghettos of Poland would well understand the meaning, and the certain effects, of such patronizing hostility.[4]

Today more Christians are martyred each year than were martyred in A.D. 100. Regent University conducted a study and concluded that nearly 156,000 Christians were martyred around the world in 1998. An estimated 164,000 were martyred in 1999.[5] Millions suffer not because of their political leanings, national affiliation, or ethnic appearance—but because they believe in Christ.

In China, Pastor Wang-Mingdao spent twenty-two years and ten months in Chinese prisons because he refused to renounce his faith. Finally, out of concern for his wife's health, he wrote a confession renouncing Christianity.

After that he was immediately released from prison. But he roamed the streets of Shanghai saying to himself, "I am Peter. I have denied my Lord." Unable to live with his remorse, he went back and recanted his denial. He was sentenced to life in prison in the 1950s. In 1980 he was released an old man, both blind and sick, but still firm in his faith. He died in 1992.[6]

Mary's wrist is badly scarred. At one time it had a cross tattooed on it as a statement of faith. Now it reminds this young Egyptian girl of the brutal kidnapping, rape, and nine-month captivity she endured at the hands of Islamic fundamentalists. They sought to force Mary into conversion to Islam. Part of the process involved her captors pouring sulfuric acid on her wrists to remove any symbol of her faith.[7]

Paul Marshall is a professor, columnist, and expert on religious persecution who has testified on persecution before the U.S. Congress. He eloquently describes these persecuted Christians:

> [They] are African women who rise at dawn to greet the rising sun in a wailing chant of thanks to God. They are Indian untouchables clearing up the excrement from the streets. They are slaves in Sudanese markets. They are Chinese peasants flip-flopping by the rice fields or pedaling bicycles through Shanghai. They are Mexican tribal people driven from their ancestral homes. They are Filipino maids, misused throughout the world. They are Russian Orthodox priests, hit by cars which mysteriously careen onto the sidewalk. . . . And, overwhelmingly, they are a people who, given a moment's time, space, and freedom, live life with joy, enthusiasm, and gratitude.[8]

These are people who know what it is to rejoice amid terrible circumstances. Their hope sustains them. Their

113

stories break our hearts. We long to do something, and we can: We can pray. This is what they ask us to do and this is what we can do. Hebrews 13:3 tells us: "Remember those in prison as if you were their fellow prisoners, and those who are mistreated as if you yourselves were suffering." Paul concludes his letter to the Colossians by saying, "Remember my chains. Grace be with you" (Col. 4:18).

Millions have paid dearly for their faith since Jesus spoke that day on the hillside. The persecuted understand pain in ways I do not understand. They know what it is to look forward to their reward.

## Struggle of a Lifetime

Peter puts persecution into perspective:

> Who is going to harm you if you are eager to do good? But even if you should suffer for what is right, you are blessed. "Do not fear what they fear; do not be frightened." But in your hearts set apart Christ as Lord. Always be prepared to give an answer to everyone who asks you to give the reason for the hope that you have. But do this with gentleness and respect, keeping a clear conscience, so that those who speak maliciously against your good behavior in Christ may be ashamed of their slander. It is better, if it is God's will, to suffer for doing good than for doing evil.
>
> 1 PETER 3:13–17

Jesus says this persecution comes because of whom we represent. There is great joy in representing such an awesome God and in sharing in the sufferings of Christ.

William Wilberforce, who lived in the eighteenth and nineteenth centuries in England, knew this joy. Though he is relatively unknown in America, he is widely known in England as the single most influential person in stopping slavery. He was elected to the Parliament at the age of twenty-one, and he found himself up against the struggle of a lifetime. When he became a Christian, he knew that his beliefs were directly opposed to the slave trade and he thought of quitting Parliament. But John Newton, a converted slave trader who wrote the hymn "Amazing Grace," encouraged him to stay in politics.

One day Wilberforce took the floor of Parliament and introduced a bill for the abolition of the slave trade. He talked for four and a half hours, but the bill was shot down. The next year he did it again and he was defeated. For more than two decades he took the floor, year after year, fighting for the cause of righteousness. After twenty years of struggle, in 1807, the vote was cast and the slave trade was abolished. At the announcement of the vote, the Parliament jumped up and applauded so loudly and for so long that it is considered to be one of the greatest ovations ever given in its history. Wilberforce was so overwhelmed that he sat there with his face in his hands and wept.

But the battle was not over. Though the slave trade was abolished, Wilberforce would spend the next twenty-five years battling to emancipate existing slaves. He became the object of ridicule in every kind of cartoon. Threats were made on his life, and he had to hire bodyguards. Attacks came from the newspapers, from friends, and from associates. He was accused of beating his wife and of secretly marrying a black woman. Just three months before his death, he was still out campaigning for petitions to emancipate current slaves. He said, "I had never thought to appear in public again, but it shall never be said that William Wilberforce is silent while the slaves require his help."[9]

115

Wilberforce also fought valiantly for the rights of single mothers, orphans, soldiers, and sailors. Fifty-nine years after his first article on slavery, he came to the end of his life. He resigned from Parliament and on his deathbed received word that the vote was cast. Seven hundred thousand British slaves had been set free. A few days later he died. What an example of a person who did the right thing regardless of the cost!

## Suffering Produces Hope

Paul writes:

> Therefore, since we have been justified through faith, we have peace with God through our Lord Jesus Christ, through whom we have gained access by faith into this grace in which we now stand. And we rejoice in the hope of the glory of God. Not only so, but we also rejoice in our sufferings, because we know that suffering produces perseverance; perseverance, character; and character, hope. And hope does not disappoint us, because God has poured out his love into our hearts by the Holy Spirit, whom he has given us.
>
> ROMANS 5:1–5

Paul uses three words that capture a Christian's experience. He says we have *peace* with God in Jesus; we have *grace* on which we stand by faith and *glory* based on our hope. Peace, grace, and glory, rooted in faith and hope, characterize the Christian life. John Stott wrote: "In the word 'peace' we look back to the enmity which is now over. In the word 'grace' we look up to our reconciled Father in whose favor we now continue to stand. In the word 'glory' we look on to our final destiny, seeing and reflecting the glory of God, which is the object of our hope or expectation."[10]

Paul links our sufferings and our future glory with the element of rejoicing, which binds the two. "We rejoice in the hope of the glory of God" and "we rejoice in our sufferings." We know that suffering serves as a means to an end—experiencing the glory of God. "We share in his [Jesus'] sufferings in order that we may also share in his glory" (Rom. 8:17).

*Suffering* means "pressed together." We are pressured through troubles, which produce endurance. Endurance results in patience, a sense of bearing the weight of circumstances. Paul writes about "endurance inspired by hope in our Lord Jesus Christ" (1 Thess. 1:3). Endurance produces character. The word *character* was used to refer to the testing of precious metals to discover or demonstrate their purity. Suffering proves our character—the genuine nature of our faith and hope.

We know this hope won't disappoint us or humiliate and embarrass us. It won't let us down. We know this because of God's love. Our hope rests on the loving character of God, which is the basis for our confidence. He has attested to this by pouring out his Holy Spirit into our hearts, confirming his love.

## Hope for the Brokenhearted

Remember your first broken heart? I do. I can't remember her name, but I can see her face as if it were yesterday. One day in elementary school as I was walking to class, I noticed she was giggling with her friends behind me. Each time I turned around, she would wave and smile and blush. *Hey, she likes me,* I thought. *She likes me a lot.*

117

*She is head over heels in love with me!* So I made the cardinal schoolboy mistake. I asked a friend of hers to ask her if she would be known as my girlfriend. (I was too young to know what this meant, but I thought it sounded mature.) I waited for the answer with such anticipation I didn't sleep at all that night.

The answer finally came: no, a word so bold, so decisive, so hard. This was my first broken heart, and I was over it within a day or two. Don't you wish all broken hearts could heal as easily as those in elementary school? But broken hearts can be devastating. The pain of a broken marriage, a broken home, a broken life does not easily go away. For years afterward the wounds are real and the scars still visible.

There is hope, encouragement, and comfort for those who are brokenhearted. There are people all around who have been so overwhelmed by life, whose hearts have been crushed so profoundly, they feel there is no hope. They wonder if they could ever be comforted; they feel as if their grief will take them to their graves.

The Bible commands us to rejoice in persecution, which drives home the fact that biblical joy is independent of immediate circumstances and grounded in future hope. The principle applies to those facing persecution or any difficult circumstance. Between what happens to us and how we respond, we always have the freedom to choose. In spite of great suffering we can choose happiness in God and look forward to the future with hope. (We will talk more about the power of hope in chapter 8.) Each day the choice is ours. We might *be* victims of terrible acts, but *living* as victims is our choice.

More than twenty-five years ago, Tim Hansel dug his mountain-climbing snow boots into a palisade glacier on the Sierra range. His nickname was Thrasher, a name he had earned because of the aggressive way he climbed. The night before, his group had slept on the mountain and planned to climb to fourteen thousand feet on this day. As the climbers began to alternate leads, the risk of a fall grew greater. Still, any experienced climber could always do a "self-arrest" with his ax if he began to fall. Yet on this particular day, when Tim lost his footing, gravity put his ax just out of reach. He began to fall at a rate of thirty-two feet per second.

When he regained consciousness, he lay on a ledge far down the mountain. His fellow climbers thought he was dead. As he began to check his body, he was amazed to discover that nothing was broken. He walked on his own back down to the vehicles and headed home. For three days he felt fine—just a little shorter. During the fourth night he woke up in unbelievable pain. For three days his body had been in complete shock.

Today, all these years later, Tim may go ten weeks at a time without sleeping a full night. Many times he can't even reach down to his knees because of the constant arthritis and disorientation of his joints. If anyone has a right to be completely unhappy, it's Tim Hansel. But he considers every day a gift.

Tim Hansel wrote:

For years, people have asked me, "Haven't you prayed to the Lord for healing?"
My obvious answer: "Of course."
"Why hasn't he healed you?"
"He has."
"But I thought you were still in pain."
"I am."
"I don't understand."

119

"I have prayed hundreds, if not thousands, of times for the Lord to heal me—and he finally *healed me of the need to be healed*. I . . . discovered a peace inside the pain. . . . I've survived because I've discovered a new and different kind of joy that I never knew existed—a joy that can coexist with uncertainty and doubt, pain, confusion and ambiguity."[11]

Tim's is a powerful story of discovering real peace, joy, and happiness in the midst of great trial. When I read of his experience, it had a profound impact on me. Tim taught me that true happiness is more than just a feeling, more than a passing moment of bliss, more than an emotional state. True happiness is part of a transformation from the inside out that occurs as we hope in God.

Some of you are dealing with situations so painful it is a life-and-death struggle to choose joy at each moment, much less each day. Maybe you are grieving the loss of a loved one, and you find yourself fighting back the tears several times a day. Maybe you are facing a terminal illness, and the emotional and physical pain is tearing you apart. Maybe your job is so stressful that you are living on the ragged edge and coming unglued. Understand that it is healthy to grieve and reach out for help. Remember the adage: Pain is inevitable; misery is optional.

I wish I could shelter you from pain. I wish I could make the sickness go away. I wish I could bring your loved one back. But I can't. You can't. But you can choose whether the pain leads to misery or not. Put your trust in God. Reach out to him and choose to open your heart to his healing, transforming power. He loves you more in your pain than you can ever understand. He has promised that a day will come when your pain will fade into the joy of heaven.

## Questions for Discussion

1. What is the worst physical pain you have ever experienced?
2. Romans 5:3–5 reads: "We also rejoice in our sufferings, because we know that suffering produces perseverance; perseverance, character; and character, hope. And hope does not disappoint us." How does this verse teach that suffering inspires hope?
3. Why do you think the Bible tells us to rejoice in our suffering?
4. Have you ever seen someone left out or criticized for his or her faith at school, work, or home? What happened?
5. When Jesus says, "Blessed are the persecuted," what does he mean?
6. How can joy be independent of circumstances?

# SEVEN

# A HOPE THAT FACES FEAR

*The greatest weakness of all is the great fear of appearing weak.*[1]

JACQUES-BÉNIGNE BOSSUET

Not long after watching *Jaws*, my family went on a vacation to the southern coast of Texas. I was about ten years old. One day, swimming in the Gulf of Mexico, the tide took me out farther than I should have been. As I swam back toward the shore, I suddenly saw what looked like a shark fin about twenty feet away from me. All the images of the movie came to me in a flash. I saw myself being thrown around like a rag doll in the water, then limping up to the shore with one leg. There would be TV cameras, helicopters, search and rescue units. The headline would read: VACATION TURNS TRAGIC. Then, my funeral. It would be a beautiful funeral—my parents crying and everybody talking about what a loss it was.

My fear came out in a scream. Floating on an air mattress a short distance away, my older sister, who was in her twenties, heard me and headed in my direction. Peter would have been impressed if he had seen me get on my sister's air mattress—I walked on water for a solid ten feet before I made it onto the float.

My heart was racing, my pulse pounding in my throat. After a moment's relief, I realized we were on an air mattress—an *air mattress!* My funeral image now included my sister! We paddled with all our might. We wanted to escape the shark, but we were terrified to put our hands in the water for more than a millisecond. The fin circled us. Music from *Jaws* began playing in my mind.

When we were close enough to the beach area to be heard, I yelled, "Shark! Shark! Run for your lives!" Everybody looked at me and then resumed what they were doing. "Shark," I yelled, wondering if these people were deaf, brain dead, or if they just hadn't seen the movie yet.

A buff surfer guy swam to me. "Shark! Shark!" I spurted out between breaths.

His eyes moved across the water. Then he began laughing. "That's not a shark," he said. "It's a dolphin. He wants to play."

A dolphin?

Then Mr. Know-It-All-of-the-Ocean proceeds to swim out, grab the dolphin's tail, and "play" with the dolphin. I felt that mixed emotion of relief and foolishness. The amazing thing was that even though my sister and I were having a panic attack, the rest of the people were enjoying the waves. You can be ten feet from someone going to pieces with fear and feel entirely peaceful. After that event, I stayed on the beach—I'd had enough water for the day. Fear comes in all shapes and sizes, from shark-sized to goldfish-sized. For example, here are some phobias I have observed:

*Homilophobia:* Fear of sermons. I am sure this does not apply to anyone in your church!

*Phronemophobia:* Fear of thinking. Think about that!

*Scolionophobia:* Fear of school. Be glad your kid does not know I've coined a term for this!

*Syngenesophobia:* Fear of relatives. You might feel this more acutely during the holidays.

For many years a bee could cause me to panic. I had been stung one too many times as a child—the swelling, the pain, the trauma. So I admit it, "My name is Jud Wilhite, and I have apiphobia (fear of bees)."

**Fear Factor**

We call fear by many names—worry, tension, anxiety, stress. Since fear is part of our body's natural alarm system, not all fear is bad. It tells us when to be careful, when to check our backs. Fear causes us to protect ourselves from danger. But many people experience an unhealthy fear. Fear has tremendous power over us; we are all afraid of something. Fear has a way of paralyzing us, draining the joy out of life, and reducing healthy expectation of the future to anxiety. In fact some of the most universal fears involve the fear of death and the fear of failure.

### Fear of Death

Gianni Versace faced his greatest fear on July 15, 1997, the day he was murdered. The famous fashion designer lived a luxurious life. Even singer/actress Madonna said she was embarrassed by how much money he spent. Versace's Florida home was estimated to be worth about forty million dollars. He had servants from Sri Lanka wearing white-laced gloves to take care of his every need. When Versace was once asked if he believed in God, he responded, "Yes, I believe in God, but I'm not the kind of religious person who goes to church, who believes in the fairy tale of Jesus born in the stable with the donkey. . . . I'm not stupid. I can't believe that God, with all the power that he has, had to have himself born in a stable. It wouldn't have been comfortable."[2]

When Versace walked out of his home that fateful day, he was shot down. He had once said to his biographer, "I'd like to live forever. If there's one thing I'm afraid of, it's missing what will happen tomorrow." Unfortunately Versace's fear was realized.

Fear of missing what happens tomorrow is one of life's universal fears. Some face this fear by creating an enduring legacy. The Egyptians faced it by constructing great pyramids that would outlive their time. Some seek fame and believe their name will live on in lights. Science holds out hope with cryonics, the practice of freezing a person's body so that it can be resuscitated in the future. Our tendency is to deny death, delay it, or try to think positively about it, but the underlying fear remains for most people.

126

### Fear of Failure

Not only do we fear death but we fear failure. Whether it is failure at work or relational failure, we go to almost every length imaginable to avoid it. Parents know the fear of failure. Remember before you had kids when you'd say, "My child will never do that. What's wrong with those parents?" Then your child collapses on the floor of the grocery store and throws a walleyed fit. Now here you are and your kid is going nuts and all the other parents are staring at you. Suddenly you feel like all your fears of failing as a parent are being realized.

## Fear and Hope

When we don't get the promotion, make a critical mistake on the sports team, or struggle in our marriage, the fear of rejection can grip us. Fear of the unknown can paralyze us with questions: What if I lose my job? What if I am injured? What if one of my kids is hospitalized and we don't have the money to cover the bills? What if my investments fail? What if my business goes under? These shark-sized fears circle us.

There is a connection that runs throughout the Bible linking fear and hope. Hope gives perspective and insight to fear. David writes: "The eyes of the LORD are on those who fear him, on those whose hope is in his unfailing love" (Ps. 33:18). When the Bible speaks of "fearing" God, it means a reverent fear, not a panic fear. We revere God because he is awesome and mighty. When we orient ourselves to him, we are able to combat our fears properly. The greater our realization of God, the smaller our fears appear.

### Hope, Fear, and God's Name

In college I had a professor who had an amazing knowledge of the biblical meaning of names. At the end of class, students would tell him their names and he'd relate the biblical meaning. He'd say things like, "Your name means awesome servant" or "mighty warrior."

After watching this go on after class a few times I thought, *This is cool. I'm going to find out what my name means.* So I approached him and asked, "What does Judson mean?" I waited with expectation. He had to look it up in his books. I anticipated hearing something profound like "Judson means incredible communicator" or "great pastor/leader." Instead, he came back and said, "Judson technically means son of Jud."

I paused and tried to think of an inspiring spin I could put on that meaning. I quickly gave up. "That's it?" I asked. "Nothing great or world changing? Just son of Jud?"

"I'm afraid that's it," he said. And there went my hopes of someone ever making a key chain out of my name.

Although my name is not impressive, God's name is. God is concerned about his name because it represents who he is. When God appeared to Moses at the burning bush, he revealed his name: "I AM WHO I AM." He is the great I AM, the one who always has been, always is, and always will be. In a world in which the markets change, neighborhoods change, relationships change, and people change, God is eternal. His name is holy.

In the Bible we read of the seraphim, angelic beings, singing to one another, "Holy, holy, holy is the LORD Almighty; the whole earth is full of his glory" (Isa. 6:3). Heaven's praise continues day and night, "Holy, holy, holy is the Lord God Almighty, who was, and is, and is to come" (Rev. 4:8).

We often miss the meaning of the triple repetition of God's holiness. This is a literary technique in Hebrew used for emphasis.[3] Only one attribute of God is elevated to the third degree. God is not just holy; he is not even holy, holy. He is holy, holy, holy. As R. C. Sproul says, "The Bible never says that God is love, love, love; or mercy, mercy, mercy; or wrath, wrath, wrath; or justice, justice, justice. It does say that he is holy, holy, holy, that the whole earth is full of his glory."[4]

When *holy* describes God, it is a synonym for all his attributes. Holiness contains the idea of moral purity, but it extends beyond to encompass all that God is. *Holy* sets him apart as the all-knowing, all-present Creator and Sustainer of the cosmos.[5]

To hope in and fear God's name is to cling to everything that he is as a holy, eternal being. In God we have all things. When suffering comes, we cling to him. When blessings come, we praise him. When challenges come, we depend on him. He is our righteousness when we fail and our strength when we are weak. He is our power when we are powerless and our wisdom when we are lost. We can place our trust in his name. As we revere his name and cling to him, our fear of worldly things is put into perspective.

The psalmist writes: "God is our refuge and strength. . . . Therefore we will not fear" (Ps. 46:1–2). Moses introduced the concept of God as a refuge after a critical victory. The Israelites had warred with the Amalekites in a bitter feud. During the heat of battle, Moses held his hands up in prayer, and the Israelites began to win. When he lowered his hands, the Amalekites threatened to defeat them. Eventually, when Moses could hold his arms up no longer,

Aaron and Hur held his hands for him as he prayed. Because of their reliance on God, they won the victory.

After the battle Moses built an altar and named it "The LORD is my Banner" (Exod. 17:15). This name has great significance. When someone raised a banner in battle, it signified that they were not defeated. Hope still existed. They were still in the fight. People would rally to the person holding the banner. The banner was a refuge because of the strength and security found as people gathered around it. When Moses named God "The LORD is my Banner," or Jehovah Nissi, he was saying that God is his rally point and protection. The Greek translation of Jehovah Nissi is literally "Lord my refuge." God was his stronghold and fortress where he found protection.

Just as Moses lifted his hands in prayer and God brought the victory, we can allow God to fight our battles. Prayer has an amazing ability to bring insight into our situation and allow us to tap into a power far beyond our own. We see Jesus praying in some of the most difficult situations—before choosing the twelve disciples, before being arrested. He called out to his Father who empowered him to overcome his fears.

Too often prayer is practiced only in times of desperation. How many times have you prayed before a test for which you were not ready? I had a Bible professor in college who prayed before tests: "Lord, bless each student according to the level of his or her preparation." Ouch!

We pray in times of desperation, but we underestimate the power of prayer for every day, every circumstance, every situation, every fear. Through prayer God parted the waters of the Red Sea; he brought fire from heaven to help Elijah; he overthrew armies and caused the sun to stand still; he raised the dead. If he can do all those things and many more in response to prayer, he can handle our fears!

According to Herbert Locklear, Scripture offers 650 definite prayers, exclusive of the Psalms, and at least 450 have definite answers. In the act of prayer we acknowledge that we are weak and God is strong. We admit that we cannot go through life alone and that we do not have to. The Lord our Banner, our Refuge, is an ever-present help in times of need. What are you afraid of? Take it to God in prayer.

## Hope's Refuge

I picked up a copy of *The Worst-Case Scenario Survival Handbook: Travel*. The book explains what to do in life's worst-case travel scenarios, like how to stop a runaway train, break free from the trunk of a car, survive a volcanic eruption, escape a high-rise hotel fire, crash-land a plane on water, and live to tell the tale of a runaway camel. There's even a section on how to foil a UFO abduction.

I don't put much faith in UFO sightings and extraterrestrial hype, but if, by some worst-case scenario, an extraterrestrial biological entity (EBE) does attempt to abduct you, here's what to do—according to the handbook: "Step 1: Do not panic." The book says the EBE might sense your fear and act rashly. So, if an alien shows up at your door and by some miracle of God you don't panic, here's the next step: "Control your thoughts. Do not think of anything violent or upsetting—the EBE may have the ability to read your mind. Try to avoid mental images of abduction; . . . such images may encourage them to take you."

Here you are being abducted by an alien, and the handbook says you should think happy thoughts. Say to yourself, *I'm running through the fields to the* Sound of Music; *I'm not going for an eternal ride on a saucer; I'm not being abducted by an otherworldly creature who will probe my body and discard me when finished!*

If the EBE attacks you, "Physical resistance should be used only as a last resort. Go for the EBE's eyes (if they have any)."[6]

I'm not sure the *Worst-Case Scenario Survival Handbook* will be much help in a crisis, but occasionally most of us find ourselves in some tough situations. Maybe it is an illness, the loss of a friend, a teenager out of control, marriage on the rocks, a midlife crisis, a retirement that wasn't what we thought it would be. Where do we turn when we find ourselves in a worst-case scenario in life? Where do we turn when our most charming charm and our best ideas fail us?

The Bible tells us where we can turn in worst-case scenarios. It says that in our fears and struggles "we who have taken refuge" should lay "hold of the hope set before us" and be greatly encouraged (Heb. 6:18 NASB). The idea of fleeing for refuge brings back images of the Old Testament cities of refuge.

In the Old Testament, God commanded the Israelites to set up six cities of refuge. Most were in the hill country, cities with lights visible at night. God singled out these cities as places of public access and hope. They were spread out evenly through Israel so that nobody was too far from one at any given time. The city of refuge was a place to flee for someone who was accused of a crime that he or she did not commit. The cities also served as a safe place for someone who committed an unintentional murder. In these situations, the blood avenger, the nearest living relative of the one slain, would come after the person who had caused the death. So the accused fled to the city of refuge.

Around the city there were bridges over ravines so that a person could quickly access it. The city had a supply of food and water, and the city gates were never locked. When a person fled to a city of refuge, he or she would be safe until the details of what had happened were worked out. The cities of refuge are a picture of Jesus. His door is never locked; he is accessible and available to us in times of trouble. We flee to Jesus who is our hope, our refuge from guilt, condemnation, judgment, self-hatred, inadequacy, despair, hopelessness, and oppression. We are safe in Jesus. He shields us from the penalty our sins deserve. He offers us the amazing "hope of eternal life, which God, who does not lie, promised before the beginning of time" (Titus 1:2). He protects us under his mercy.

## God's Control

Hope rests on God's ability to control the future. Paul writes of a time when he and his associates were under great hardship in Asia. It got so difficult they even despaired of life. Have you ever been there? Maybe when the pregnancy test came back negative again, when your teenager ran away, when your spouse was diagnosed with cancer, when your child went to the ER, when you lost your job?

Even though Paul and his friends felt a death sentence, he says, "On him [God] we have set our hope that he will continue to deliver us" (2 Cor. 1:10). The idea of setting one's hope on God is predominant throughout the Bible. At the end of the day we face our fears by placing our hope in him. We may face great difficulties in life, but even in the midst of them we set our hope on God and trust that he is in control. When we struggle and are weary and worn, we set our hope on him. When the market collapses, we set our hope on him. When a teenager slams his bedroom door and says, "I hate you," we set our hope on him. When a spouse says, "I don't love you anymore," we set our hope on him. He can and will deliver us as we trust him.

When we set our hope on God, we are empowered to face our fears. The words "Do not be afraid" appear often in the Bible. When the angel Gabriel appeared to Mary, he said, "Do not be afraid" (Luke 1:30). When Jesus' followers came to look for him at the tomb after his crucifixion, they met an angelic being who reassured them, "Do not be afraid" (Matt. 28:5). Moments later they met Jesus. His first words to them were, "Greetings. . . . Do not be afraid" (vv. 9–10). You may be terrified by shark-sized fears today. As their fins circle you, the temptation to panic may be great. Place your trust in Jesus. His words to you are "Do not be afraid."

A little girl once asked her father, "Daddy, how big is God?" Her father thought for a moment and answered, "Honey, he is always bigger than you need." No matter what we are afraid of or what we are up against, God is always bigger than we need. He is bigger than our fears and our failures. With him as our guide, the greatest shark-sized fears are under control. We may find that what circles us is harmless, like the dolphin, or even better, a blessing in disguise. Set your hope on him!

## Questions for Discussion

1. Recall a time you were afraid as a child.
2. What are some ways people normally deal with fear?

3. How can hoping in God's name help us face our fears?
4. What lessons do we learn from Moses and the victory the Israelites won over the Amalekites?
5. God instructed Israel to identify cities of refuge in the Old Testament. Do you think this concept has anything to do with Jesus being our refuge? What does this image imply?
6. Share some practical ways you can set your hope on God for the future.

# EIGHT

# A HOPE THAT INSPIRES BOLDNESS

*If you ask me what I have come to do in this world . . . I will reply: I'm here to live my life OUT LOUD.*[1]

ÉMILE ZOLA

Bill Duncan walked the trenches of Vietnam as a Marine, boldly sharing the most important message of his life. Seeing one young man who had both legs and a portion of his arm blown off, he approached him.

"Do you have a cigarette?" the man asked Bill.

"Sure," Bill replied as he gave him one. Since the wounded man's nerve endings were numb, he remained coherent.

"You don't think I am going to live, do you?" the man asked.

"I don't think you are going to live here," Bill answered with great empathy, "but you can live with Christ."

Bill proceeded to share how the man could be forgiven and live with the hope of heaven. Shortly after Bill shared Jesus with him, the man died. In the trenches of war, Bill prayed for the dying, comforted the wounded, and encouraged the frightened. He was a tremendous leader and soldier who was also a radically committed Christ-follower, inspired by hope to share his faith.

Bill had entered the Marine Corps after high school graduation, and two years later he married his childhood sweetheart, Arlene. He rose through the ranks to become a colonel with some of the highest security clearances possible. During his career he lived in more than forty countries and traveled to more than eighty. He left his blood on three continents and still carries shrapnel in his body as a reminder.

After thirty years with the Marine Corps, Bill retired. He went into general contracting work and consulting, but God was preparing to use him even more dramatically. When Bill learned of great humanitarian needs in Prague, he decided to take action. He made some calls to pharmaceutical companies and arranged for medical supplies to be donated to a hospital there.

In the dead of winter he flew into Frankfurt and boarded a train to Prague. He arrived very early in the morning, but because of a miscommunication he had no contact or place to stay. Carrying five bags of valuable medical supplies, he was a prime target for thieves at the train station. So he headed into the night, searching for a place to sleep. Unable to carry all five bags at once, he leap-frogged the heavy bags about two miles on foot: dragging two bags and then turning around, while the others were in sight, and dragging them. Finally, after two miles and several attempts at knocking on doors, he found a place that would let him in. The next morning he got the medical supplies to the hospital. It was then that his vision began to expand to see ways to help the whole former Soviet Union.

Bill's vision was realized in the founding of the Commonwealth of Independent States Church Development Foundation (CDF). Bill talked with the staffs of several churches and proposed a plan to go into Minsk in Belarus with humanitarian aid and Bibles. His strategy was simple: Find the needs and seek to meet them with the love of Christ. In seven years CDF:

- sent more than one million Bibles to Belarus
- delivered 1.8 million dollars worth of medical supplies yearly
- distributed more than sixteen tons of food
- distributed thousands of dollars worth of clothing
- distributed hundreds of library book sets, which were given to churches, schools, hospitals, prisons, youth camps, and public offices

Also Bill and a team of local ministers and lay leaders assembled a manual to train prison chaplains in Belarus. They have trained more than one hundred chaplains to work with prisoners. Leading training sessions for women, they helped them find their place in ministry and recover their self-esteem. CDF was also part of the effort to start crisis pregnancy centers in Minsk.

As Bill's vision became a reality, CDF has literally changed an entire country of ten million people by meeting needs at every level of society.[2]

## Hope and Boldness

What gives a person courage to walk the trenches of battle and share Jesus? What empowers someone to go straight into the heart of once-enemy territory and boldly share his faith? What allows Bill to confront difficult situations again and again without losing heart? Bill's inspiration stems from a radical confidence in Jesus, a passion for evangelism, and an unshakable hope.

Hope empowers us to be bold in showing and sharing our faith appropriately. When we realize that our future is secure and our present is empowered, we live with renewed passion and fervor. Paul writes that we are bold because we have this hope. Just before making this statement, he contrasts the law, which came on tablets through Moses, with the Holy Spirit, who writes God's law on our hearts. Paul says, "The letter kills, but the Spirit gives life" (2 Cor. 3:6). The law diagnosed the problem of sin, but the Spirit offers a solution and empowers us to live righteously.

Hope is a certain realization that we will go from glory to glory, being transformed into the image of Jesus. Paul uses the term *glory* ten times in this section of the Bible. Glory means "tribute or honor." The term describes God's visible presence, the beauty of his character reflected in a bright countenance. When God's Spirit dwells in us, we reflect the glory of God in a way that lasts. To illustrate this, Paul writes about Moses, who spent forty days with God and received the Ten Commandments. When he came down from the mountain, his face glowed with the glory of God. After Moses spoke to the people, he put a veil over his face. The veil was necessary not only because his face was too bright to look at but also because Moses did not want the people to see the glory fading. Moses' glory

140

faded, but the Christian's glory does not fade; it lasts. Paul says the old covenant *came* with glory (past tense), but the new covenant *will be* with glory (see vv. 7–11).

A Christian's glory lasts because it is internal not external. The Ten Commandments were written in stone, but as the Holy Spirit dwells in our hearts, writing his law there, our lives are changed. The Old Testament law frustrated us because we could not keep it; the Spirit now dwells in us to initiate change. We radiate the glory of God. Paul compares the old with the new by writing: "And if what was fading away came with glory, how much greater is the glory of that which lasts! Therefore, since we have such a hope, we are very bold" (vv. 11–12).

As we surrender to God's Spirit within us, we move from glory to glory; our confidence propels us. The term *bold* referred to a citizen's right to free speech and included his or her responsibility to live within the bounds of that freedom. It could be translated "confident, frank, or public." Followers of Christ are propelled by hope to be bold in influencing others in word and deed.

## The Influence of One

While growing up, I wanted more than anything to be Tony Dorsett, the famous running back for the Dallas Cowboys. I wanted to walk like him, talk like him, look like him, and play football like him. I spent Sunday afternoons dodging imaginary players around the house in Dallas Cowboy football pads. It never occurred to me that I was a flat-footed, lanky kid who couldn't run!

As time passed, I grew out of my Tony Dorsett phase and entered into the dump truck phase. The coolest job in the world had to be driving a dump truck and having fun with everybody's trash. Then there was the TV show *CHiPs*. I wanted to be Ponch. After each episode, I would patrol the neighborhood on my bike, which, of course, I thought of as my motorcycle. The streets were safe with me on duty. Superman even captured my interest for a brief time, until one fateful day when I jumped off a ten-foot stack of wood, thinking I was actually going to fly. After landing face first on the ground, I decided Superman was not for me. From then on I settled for the Six Million Dollar Man!

It is amazing to reflect on all the people who have influenced our lives—parents, teachers, mentors, friends, bullies, leaders, enemies, athletes, celebrities, and so on. They have all influenced us in various ways. Some of them have added richness to our lives, others poison.

Whether we are aware of it or not, we influence people around us. Statistics tell us that even introverts will influence approximately ten thousand other people in an average lifetime. Each of us has a unique circle of influence, a unique network of friends, family members, and acquaintances. How do we influence them? Does our lifestyle mark their lives for good? Will our hope have an impact on them?

The influence of one person can be tremendous. At a rehearsal dinner for a wedding, I sat next to a young attorney. We began to talk about Christianity. He took a drink and said, "I always had this stereotype of a Christian as an overweight person with disheveled hair, crooked teeth, and bad breath. I thought they were all hypocrites and Christianity was a joke. Then I met someone who blew all my stereotypes out of the water."

He continued to tell me how his coworker had come into a relationship with Jesus and was now going to seminary at night to become a minister. "Jesus is so real in his life," he said. Since that time, the man had begun to read the Bible for himself and he has read several books on the Christian faith. He is not a Christian yet, but he is open because someone did more than talk about Jesus; someone's lifestyle revealed hope.

## Showing Jesus

Each Friday a special group of influencers meets at their church. They meet in Christ-centered support groups for people struggling with addictions on every level. They are people from all walks of life who have discovered hope in Jesus. One particular Friday night Rudy, a regular attendee, was absent. Rudy had lived a hard life and spent time in prison, but that was the past. He had remained clean and sober for five years and was an inspiration to others. Yet Rudy was struggling with some deep-seated issues that he had hidden from the group.

His mom had phoned someone in the recovery group earlier to share her concern. Rudy had slipped into a depression, and she feared he was suicidal. All of this heightened the group's concern when he didn't come to the meeting.

The group circled up and prayed. After a few minutes, someone's cell phone rang. Normally a ringing phone during prayer would have been annoying, but this time it felt more like a message from God. A mutual friend and co-worker of Rudy's had remembered him mentioning something about a hotel in Fullerton, California. Immediately the group thanked God for answering their prayers. They found the hotel number and called.

The hotel refused to tell them if Rudy was there. So they loaded up in a car and headed to Fullerton, a good hour away, on a wing and a prayer. When they arrived, the desk clerk still would not confirm or deny Rudy's presence. The group chose to be bold.

They began to walk the halls calling, "Rudy! Rudy!" They yelled for him in the courtyard, searched in the stairwells, and covered every inch of the hotel. Eventually a door opened and out stepped Rudy. A stunned and confused look came over his face. "What are you guys doing here?" he asked. "We were just in the neighborhood" was the reply.

Rudy had drunk away five years of sobriety that night and had considered taking his life. His friends stayed with him all night. They rallied around him, demonstrating that the role of the church is not to kick someone when he is down but to help him get up.

One of the guys in the group was not a Christ-follower. He was so moved by the way Rudy's friends cared for him that he thought: *If this is what being a fully devoted follower of Christ is about, sign me up!* Soon he committed his life to Jesus.[3]

When we are passionate about our hope, it will show in our lives. Even the smallest acts of kindness can make an eternal difference. We radiate God's glory and leave a lasting impact on others. Jesus calls it being the salt of the earth. Salt has always had great value in human society, especially in the past. In ancient Greece, salt was called *theon*, which means "divine." The Romans believed that next to the sun there was nothing more valuable than salt. Often Roman soldiers were paid in salt, thus the expression "not worth his salt." In many ancient societies salt was used as a mark of friendship. For two people to share salt indicated a mutual responsibility to look out for one another's welfare. In numerous ways Jesus' hearers would have understood that "salt of the earth" represents a valuable commodity. The primary uses of salt in the ancient world were to preserve and season food. Farmers would rub mineral salt into meat until it penetrated and dissolved. This prevented the meat from decaying. Once salt penetrated food, it served to season it. In much the same way Christians are to be "rubbed" into culture, penetrating every aspect of life to preserve and season society. We are to show Jesus to the world by our actions.

Those of you who volunteer and work for justice in myriad situations, who labor behind the scenes, who give unselfishly of your time to help someone, who send a note of encouragement, who visit a shut-in or take a meal to a family that has lost a loved one may never receive a badge or a plaque for your efforts, but you are showing your hope with your life. People will be moved by the actions they see. Your influence for good is incalculable.

Louise Brown is a volunteer who shows her hope boldly. She heads up a ministry in her church called the Shepherd Tree. At Christmastime a tree is covered with cutout paper shepherds. Each shepherd represents a child in need. Hundreds of people pick a shepherd off the tree and buy clothing and other items for that child.

From October through December each year, Louise's life focuses on this ministry. She leads a team of eighty volunteers who help with the gifts. The children's classes in her church cut out the shepherds and color them. Volunteers from the women's ministry laminate them, and then they are placed on the tree for people to select.

Through their sacrifice and acts of service, God does amazing things. He always provides people to help when there is a need. Louise tells of a time when a mother showed up with a need after the registrations had been cut off. She asked, "Is there any way I can get my three children on? I lost my job and I could really use some help." They replied, "Sign this sheet of paper and we will see what we can do." As soon as the woman walked off, another woman walked up and said, "Are there any shepherds left? I would really love to have three." They simply handed her the piece of paper. That is how God provides. He always makes a way.

Louise said, "It is so heartrending to see these people. Some of them are eternally grateful. Their children don't have any clothes. They are wearing shorts in the dead of winter." Each time a person thanks them as they present a gift, the volunteers simply tell them to thank God—he is the reason for everything. The Shepherd Tree has caused Louise to be "a lot more giving and compassionate toward other people" and has helped her realize that we all "are witnesses for Christ through what we say and our actions." They are bringing the joy of Christ to those around them.[4]

### Sharing Jesus

Bill Exley entered my living room and introduced himself. The bags under his eyes revealed several sleepless nights. He was as pale as a ghost; his body language screamed "fatigue." A few days earlier he had been a twenty-six-year-old lawyer on top of the world, out on his own, self-sufficient, and healthy. Then his life turned upside down.

Bill grew up in the Houston area and experienced a relatively normal childhood. Early on he believed in God, but as he grew older, especially in the college years, he began to question God's existence. Being trained in law and the hard sciences, he wanted strict evidence for faith. Eventually he became an atheist.

It all made sense to Bill. People were simply organisms made up of a bunch of chemical and biological reactions. There was no greater meaning to this thing called life. Religion, and especially Christianity, was just a system for getting people to do what others wanted. It was a social and political phenomenon whereby the oppressor holds his position and the oppressed take joy in their lowly state. He agreed with Karl Marx that religion is "the opium of the people."

Bill did not begin to question his philosophy of life until his girlfriend, Jodi, entered into a faith crisis. Jodi had been close with someone who was killed in a car accident. As she wrestled with this loss, she asked Bill, "Why would God allow this to happen?"

"Because there is no God," Bill replied. The answer seemed easy enough to him. "Because there is no God"— the words began to echo in his mind.

Reflecting on the death of Jodi's friend, Bill's thoughts would not let him rest. The woman who died in the wreck was thirty-two years old. Bill realized in a powerful way that death is no respecter of persons. What really troubled him was this woman's last words. As she was lying on a rain-slick road after the accident, dying, her last words were "Pray for Nickie." Nickie was her youngest daughter who had multiple sclerosis. During the accident, Nickie's wheelchair had flown forward, striking the mother. Bill wondered, *How could someone be so selfless that her last thoughts were for someone else?* Suddenly and unexpectedly, he entered into a spiritual crisis.

Bill's emotions were so strong that he did not know how to cope. In a week's time he went from being an efficient, emotionally stable, hardworking person to a basket case. He was paralyzed by the question: Does God exist? Bill could not sleep. He could not work. For six days he

147

didn't eat a bite of food, and on the sixth day he entered my living room. A friend, Peggy Culp, had reached out to him at work and suggested he visit me for counsel. He was emotionally drained, unequipped to deal with the feelings that had taken hold of him. He was burned out and struggling with depression.

After we got the introductions out of the way, Bill looked at me and said, "Okay, Santa Claus, the Easter Bunny, Jesus Christ. Do you see where I'm coming from?"

"Sure."

"A lot of Christians believe in God the way kids believe in Santa Claus and nobody ever told them that it's not true—nobody let the cat out of the bag."

"It's true a lot of Christians don't know why they believe what they believe."

So our conversation began. We talked about philosophy, archaeology, science, and history. I encouraged Bill to read the Bible for himself, to give it an honest read. One thing was obvious: Bill was starving to be in a right relationship with God. He did not know who God is and he wasn't convinced of his existence, but he was starving to know him. He was starving for answers.

Bill didn't show up at my house by accident. Peggy had prayed for Bill regularly, asking that her relationship with him might open a door of opportunity. When it did, Peggy shared her faith with compassion and clarity. She was very bold.

When Bill left my house that night, he agreed to read the Gospel of Luke. Over the next three days he read all four Gospels. He began reading authors such as C. S. Lewis and Lee Strobel who offered reasons for faith. Soon he was eating and sleeping again. But his spiritual hunger did not diminish.

Eventually a faith developed in his heart. As he investigated the reasons to believe, he was amazed and moved. By opening his life to God he experienced the freedom and the deep, abiding happiness that only Christ can give. God brought his house of cards down, and now he was rebuilding Bill's life on the Rock. On a chilly December night, Bill was baptized, connecting with the death, burial, and resurrection of Jesus Christ. The peace that surpasses understanding flooded his life. Jodi had been a Christ-follower, and she was amazed at the changes that occurred in Bill's life.

Bill and Jodi's lives would never be the same. Soon after this, they married and began their lifelong journey together. Bill speaks of how his life changed: "Every serious decision I make, big ones, little ones—I very often find myself stopping and praying about them. I used to think people who prayed were just nuts. And now I do it all the time. So much of my life is different now—what I think about, how I act, how I react to other people around me." Bill is experiencing the power of hope.[5]

There is little as moving as the experience of seeing a person come into a relationship with Jesus. The angels of heaven rejoice! Just witnessing it places life in perspective. What a privilege we have to share our hope with boldness!

How can you share your faith? Make a list of several people you know who are not in a relationship with Jesus. This list will include fellow workers, family members, and acquaintances. Pray for these people every day and ask God to open a door for you to share your faith. You might have to wait a day or ten years for the opportunity, but, if you keep faithfully praying, God will move. These prayers also make us more aware of what is happening around us. When the door opens, we will know, and God will begin to do powerful things.[6]

I'll never forget being in a doctoral program and rooming for a week with a sixty-year-old African American. He lived in the Northwest and worked as a school principal. I was a young pastor in my late twenties, serving a church in Texas. We couldn't have been farther apart in geography, background, race, or religion. Over the course of the week I asked God to open a door for me to share with him the hope I have. I longed for an opportunity to present why I am a Christ-follower. At the end of our seminar, he invited me to have lunch with him. As we sat there, he placed his fork on the table, leaned forward, and, with the most concerned, serious look you can imagine, said, "Jud, tell me how to live my life."

I had prayed for an open door; God kicked the wall down. As I shared my hope with him, he began to nod his head. What an adventure God calls us to! What a privilege to share our hope with the hopeless, the hurting, the broken, and the confused! What a journey!

## Questions for Discussion

1. Who has been the most influential person in your spiritual life?
2. Everybody influences somebody. Name someone you influence, whether at work or home.
3. On a scale of 1 to 10, how aware are you of your influence in others' lives (1 being aware of my influence and 10 being unaware of my influence)?

    1   2   3   4   5   6   7   8   9   10

4. How does hope inspire us to show and share our faith with others?

# CONCLUSION

*Hope does not disappoint us.*

ROMANS 5:5

"Are we there yet?" You'd think after thousands of years, parents would have discovered the foolproof answer to silence that question. But parents have different opinions on how to answer. The optimists say we should answer: "Almost there, just two more minutes." Pragmatists might respond by misdirection: "Look, is that your brother bending your doll's arm backward?" Still others go for a more realistic approach: "Five more hours, honey. Remember how long it took Dad to assemble your swing set? *That* long."

Maybe we haven't come up with a good answer because it's a question adults struggle with as well.

When we suffer we wonder: *Are we there yet? How much longer?*

151

When our health fades: *Are we there yet?*

When our job doesn't deliver what we hoped it would: *Are we there yet?*

When our family breaks up: *Are we there yet?*

Hope answers with a resounding Not yet! Someday this trip called "life" will begin anew. Someday all things will appear different. And that day will be glorious, better than anything we could ever imagine here. The joy will be indescribable. No more tears, suffering, letdowns, or heartache. No more evil or pain.

But hope also answers with a whispered "yes." Hope is not only a destination; it is a journey. Hope allows us to trust God, live out of his promises, look forward to his return, purify our lives, release bitterness, endure suffering, face our fears, and share our faith boldly—*now*. Hope allows us to experience God's future *today*. We discover security in God's character, peace in his promise, and confidence in his mission *at this moment*.

Are we there yet? No, but we are on the journey. As Jesus reminds us in his last recorded words: "I am coming soon" (Rev. 22:20). So next time I'm faced with *the* travel question, I'm going to answer biblically: "Soon. We'll be there soon."

# NOTES

## Introduction

1. Jürgen Moltmann, *Theology of Hope: On the Ground and the Implications of a Christian Eschatology,* trans. James W. Leitch (New York: Harper and Row, 1965), 31.
2. Diane Sawyer, *Good Morning America,* ABC, October 1, 1999.
3. C. S. Lewis, *Mere Christianity* (New York: Macmillan, 1952), 118.

## Chapter One: A Hope That Trusts God's Character

1. Lauryn Hill, "Looking for Lauryn," *Essence,* July 2002, 90.
2. John Piper, *The Pleasures of God: Meditations on God's Delight in Being God* (Portland, OR: Multnomah, 1991), 216.
3. Harold G. Wolf, quoted in Armand Nicholi, "Hope in a Secular Age," in *Finding God at Harvard,* ed. Kelly K. Monroe (Grand Rapids: Zondervan, 1996), 118.
4. Jim Collins, *Good to Great* (New York: Harper Business, 2001), 85.
5. Eugene Peterson, *A Long Obedience in the Same Direction: Discipleship in an Instant Society* (Downers Grove, IL: InterVarsity Press, 1980), 140.
6. Moltmann, *Theology of Hope,* 20.
7. Kyle Idleman, "Imagine That," audiotape of message presented to North American Christian Convention, Columbus, Ohio, July 2003, tape 41 (Bridgeport, IL: Christian Audio Tapes).
8. A. W. Pink, *The Nature of God* (Chicago: Moody Press, 1999), 69.
9. Stephen Charnock, *The Existence and Attributes of God,* vol. 2 (Grand Rapids: Baker, 1996), 214.

10. Renate Wind, *Dietrich Bonhoeffer: A Spoke in the Wheel*, trans. John Bowden (Grand Rapids: Eerdmans, 1991), 180.

## Chapter Two: A Hope That Is Stored in Heaven

1. C. S. Lewis, *The Problem of Pain* (New York: Macmillan, 1962), 143.
2. Janet Morel, *Playing the Hand That's Dealt to You: A Guide for Parents of Children with Special Needs* (Melbourne Beach, FL: Canmore Press, 2000), 116.
3. Ibid., 118.
4. Janet Morel, personal interview.
5. Ibid.
6. Richard N. Ostling et al., "Does Heaven Exist?" *Time*, March 24, 1997, 73.
7. Ibid.
8. John MacArthur, *The Glory of Heaven* (Wheaton, IL: Crossway, 1996), 107–8.
9. Ibid., 108.
10. Adapted from Kenneth Boa, *Talk Thru the New Testament* (Wheaton, IL: Tyndale, 1981), 225, quoted in Gary Phillips and William Brown, *Making Sense of Your World from a Biblical Viewpoint* (Chicago: Moody, 1991), 149.
11. Augustine, *The City of God*, trans. Marcus Dods (New York: The Modern Library, 1993), 865.
12. Jonathan Edwards, *The Works of Jonathan Edwards*, vol. 2 (1834; reprint, Peabody, MA: Hendrickson, 2000), 620.
13. Morel interview.
14. Quoted in Philip Yancey, *Disappointment with God* (New York: Guideposts, 1988), 97.

## Chapter Three: A Hope That Anticipates Jesus' Return

1. Dag Hammarskjöld, *Markings*, quoted in Philip Yancey, *Reaching for the Invisible God* (Grand Rapids: Zondervan, 1963), 63.
2. Laura Lee, "Really Bad Predictions," *The Futurist*, September/October 2000, 20–25.
3. Quoted in Leonard Sweet, *Soul Tsunami* (Grand Rapids: Zondervan, 1999), 24.
4. Robert G. Clouse, Robert N. Hosack, and Richard V. Pierard, *The New Millennium Manual* (Grand Rapids: Baker, 1999), 112–15.
5. Ibid., 125.
6. Peterson, *Long Obedience in the Same Direction*, 139.
7. Lewis Smedes, *Keeping Hope Alive* (Nashville: Thomas Nelson, 1998), 11.
8. Quoted in Clouse, Hosack, and Pierard, *New Millennium Manual*, 177.

## Chapter Four: A Hope That Purifies Our Lives

1. C. S. Lewis, *Letters of C. S. Lewis*, ed. W. H. Lewis (New York: Harcourt and Brace, 1966), 289.

2. Augustine, *City of God,* 865.

3. John Piper, *Desiring God* (Sisters, OR: Multnomah, 1996), 22–23.

4. Dietrich Bonhoeffer, *The Cost of Discipleship,* trans. R. H. Fuller (New York: Macmillan, 1959), 125.

5. Søren Kierkegaard, *Purity of Heart Is to Will One Thing,* trans. Douglass Steere (New York: Harper and Row, 1948), 31.

6. Dallas Willard, *The Divine Conspiracy: Rediscovering our Hidden Life in God* (New York: HarperSanFrancisco, 1998), 95.

7. John MacArthur, *Romans 1–8* (Chicago: Moody, 1991), 392.

8. John Bunyan, *Pilgrim's Progress in Today's English* (Chicago: Moody, 1964), 71–72.

9. Bonhoeffer, *Cost of Discipleship,* 60.

## Chapter Five: A Hope That Releases Bitterness

1. Mel Gibson, interview on *The O'Reilly Factor,* Fox, January 16, 2003.

2. Quoted in Lee Strobel, *God's Outrageous Claims* (Grand Rapids: Zondervan, 1997), 15.

3. Ibid.

4. Frederick Buechner, *Wishful Thinking: A Theological ABC* (Harper and Row, 1973), 136.

5. Lorne Sanny, quoted in Dick Tripp, "Why Forgiveness Matters," http://www.christianity.co.nz/forgive5.htm (October 6, 2003).

6. Lewis, *Mere Christianity,* 104.

7. David Stevens, "Till Death Do Us Part," *The Upbeat Reporter,* February 2000, 4.

8. Corrie ten Boom with John Sherrill and Elizabeth Sherrill, *The Hiding Place* (Washington Depot, CN: Barbour, 1971), 125.

9. Mike Warnke, *Friendly Fire: A Recovery Guide for Believers Battered by Religion* (Shippensburg, PA: Destiny Image, 2002), 20.

10. Ibid., 160.

## Chapter Six: A Hope That Transforms Suffering

1. Kathleen Norris, *Amazing Grace* (New York: Penguin, 1998), 214.

2. The details of Jim and Lana McKee's story come from a personal interview, winter 2000.

3. John Foxe, *Foxe's Book of Martyrs* (Old Tappan, NJ: Revell, 1968), 13–14.

4. Michael Horowitz, quoted in Paul Marshall, *Their Blood Cries Out* (Dallas: Word, 1997), xxi.

5. DC Talk and the Voice of the Martyrs, *Jesus Freaks* (Tulsa, OK: Asbury, 1999), 15.

6. Marshall, *Their Blood Cries Out,* 71–72.

7. Ibid., 15–16.

8. Ibid., 9.

Bibliography notes.

9. Christopher Hancock, "The 'Shrimp' Who Stopped Slavery," *Christian History* 53 (1997): 12–19.

10. John Stott, *Men Made New: An Exposition of Romans 5–8* (Grand Rapids: Baker, 1984), 13.

11. Tim Hansel, *You Gotta Keep Dancin'* (Elgin, IL: LifeJourney Books, 1985), 123, 132.

## Chapter Seven: A Hope That Faces Fear

1. Jacques-Bénigne Bossuet, http://home.att.net/~quotations/fear.html (July 10, 2003).

2. R. Albert Mohler Jr., "Violence in Vanity Fair: The Versace Murder," *Fidelitas,* http://www.sbts.edu/mohler/Fidelitasprint.php?article=Fidel057 (February 1, 2004).

3. R. C. Sproul, *The Holiness of God* (Wheaton, IL: Tyndale, 1998), 25.

4. Ibid., 26.

5. Jud Wilhite, *Faith That Goes the Distance: Living an Extraordinary Life* (Grand Rapids: Baker, 2001), 60.

6. Joshua Piven and David Borgenicht, *The Worst-Case Scenario Survival Handbook: Travel* (San Francisco: Chronicle Books, 2001), 58.

## Chapter Eight: A Hope That Inspires Boldness

1. Émile Zola, quoted in Tom Peters, *The Circle of Innovation* (New York: Vintage, 1997), 489.

2. Bill Duncan, personal interview, winter 2000.

3. Rudy, personal interview, spring 2003.

4. Louise Brown, personal interview, winter 2000.

5. Bill Exley, personal interview, fall 1999.

6. Bill Hybels and Mark Mittelberg, *Becoming a Contagious Christian* (Grand Rapids: Zondervan, 1994).

**Jud Wilhite** is senior pastor of Central Christian Church in Henderson, Nevada, a suburb of Las Vegas. He and his wife, Lori, have two children, Emma and Ethan.

# Also by Jud Wilhite

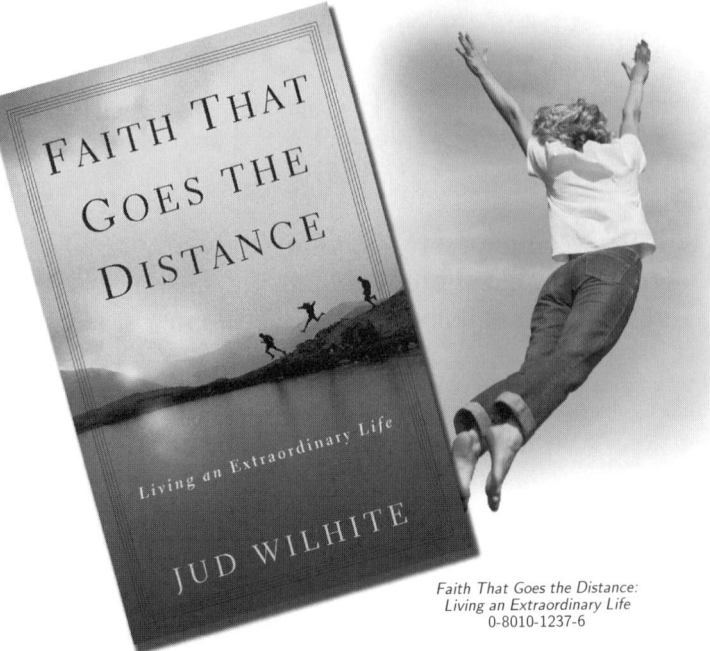

Faith That Goes the Distance:
Living an Extraordinary Life
0-8010-1237-6

## Praise for *Faith That Goes the Distance*

"An intelligent, clever, and explosive exploration of faith's power. This book speaks to the heart with wisdom and humor. Get ready to be moved as well as inspired!"
—*Barry McMurtrie, senior pastor, Crossroads Christian Church*

"This book will remind you of how God can use absolutely anyone to glorify his kingdom. Jud makes it clear, through God's Word, that you don't have to be a figure of prominence for your faith to make a difference in the lives of others. If you are willing to do the natural by taking a stand for Christ and becoming obedient to his Word, Christ will bless you with the super and lead others closer to him."
—*Brandon Slay, U. S. Olympic Gold Medalist*

"Directly ties the faith of the 'giants of the Bible' with the 'giants' that live among us today, and encourages us toward that same exercise of faith. *Faith That Goes the Distance* was worth the wait!"
—*Upbeat Reporter Book Review*

"Puts forth a clear and inspirational plan for how to live an extraordinary adventure with God. Filled with powerful stories of how God works through everyday people, *Faith That Goes the Distance* will challenge you to take a risk and discover life's greatest rewards."
—*Mike Foster, cofounder of xxxchurch.com*

# Looking for Love?
## You just found it.

"After reading *Love that Goes the Distance*, my life will never be the same—and neither will yours."
—Pat Williams, Sr. vice president, Orlando Magic

"Jud Wilhite empowers us to love when it's not easy by learning from real life experiences and Bible characters who can teach us valuable lessons."
—Bob Russell, senior minister, Southeast Christian Church

"I predict you will be giving this book away often to friends who need to be reminded of the power of supernatural love."
—Gene Appel, associate pastor, Willow Creek Community Church

## LOVE THAT GOES THE DISTANCE

Discover the Power That Conquers All

### JUD WILHITE

"Full of encouraging insights. Wilhite has taken God's truths and spilled light on them exposing God's love that has the power to transform our lives."
—Greg Nettle, senior pastor, RiverTree Christian Church, Ohio

"An inspirational read no matter where you are on the journey of life."
—Chaplain Raymond Giunta, executive director/founder of We Care Ministries